THE COMPLETE BOOK OF RUG MAKING

FOLK METHODS AND ETHNIC DESIGNS

Also by Cecelia Felcher:
The Needlepoint Workbook of Traditional Designs

THE COMPLETE BOOK OF RUG MAKING

FOLK METHODS AND ETHNIC DESIGNS

CECELIA FELCHER

Graphs by Jerome Felcher
Photographs by Daniel Quat
Drawings by Elaine Weinmann

HAWTHORN BOOKS, INC.
PUBLISHERS / *New York*

THE COMPLETE BOOK OF RUG MAKING: FOLK METHODS AND ETHNIC DESIGNS

Copyright © 1975 by Cecelia Felcher. Copyright under International and Pan-American Copyright Conventions. All rights reserved, including the right to reproduce this book or portions thereof in any form, except for the inclusion of brief quotations in a review. All inquiries should be addressed to Hawthorn Books, Inc., 260 Madison Avenue, New York, New York 10016. This book was manufactured in the United States of America and published simultaneously in Canada by Prentice-Hall of Canada, Limited, 1870 Birchmount Road, Scarborough, Ontario.

Library of Congress Catalog Card Number: 74-22927

ISBN: 0-8015-1654-4

1 2 3 4 5 6 7 8 9 10

TO

Jerry, Michael, and Robert,
whose encouragement, help,
and love were my motivation.

CONTENTS

ACKNOWLEDGMENTS   ix

INTRODUCTION   xi

HISTORY   13

HOOKED RUGS   15

History . Hooking Methods . Equipment . Preparing Foundation Fabrics or Backings . Creating Your Own Designs . Transferring Designs . Attaching to Frame . Hooking Procedures . Where to Start . Finishing . Designs

BRAIDED RUGS   61

History . Equipment . Preparation . Procedures . Finishing . Designs

PEN WIPER RUG   77

RYA RUGS   79

History . Equipment . Procedures . The Rya or Ghiordes Knot . Designs

LATCH HOOKED RUGS   93

History . Equipment . Procedures . Designs

EMBROIDERED RUGS   107

    Introduction . Equipment . Stitches . Designs

CROCHETED RUGS   141

    History . Equipment . Stitches . Designs

KNITTED RUGS   161

    History . Procedures . Designs

SIMPLE WOVEN RUGS   175

    Introduction . The Mechanics of Weaving . Equipment .
    Weaving Procedures . Rya Weaving Procedures

DYEING   180

    Introduction . Mordants . Natural Dyeing Procedures .
    Natural Dyeing Color Sources

FINISHING   199

    Blocking . Joining . Binding . Fringe . Lining . Care

BIBLIOGRAPHY   203

INDEX   205

ACKNOWLEDGMENTS

Many people were helpful during the planning and preparation of this book. I would like to thank all of my friends for their kindness during some trying days. Special thanks and appreciation must be given to Elizabeth Malament, who did most of the work for the knitting and crocheting chapters; Helen Fetzer and Betty Swezey, who proofread the braiding chapter so creatively and constructively; Daga Ramsey, whose experience with rya was extremely helpful; Florence Friedman, who made the chapter on weaving comprehensible; Alice Epstein, who approved the chapter on hooking.

I would also like to thank Danny Quat, a most patient and talented photographer; Elaine Weinmann, who not only drew the beautiful illustrations but typed as well; my husband Jerome Felcher, who made the graphs; my editor, Elizabeth Backman, whose help was indispensable; Joan Toggitt, for her generosity; Paternayan Yarns for their cooperation; Hazel Werner, for testing directions; Sandra Choron, for all her help; and Minna and Sol Zaret, Lois and Norman Schneyer, Eunice Plesser and James Abbe, Jr., for the use of their antique rugs; Port Washington Art Gallery and Egetaepper, Inc., for the use of their antique rugs; Port Washington Gallery and Egetaepper, Inc., for the use of their rugs; and to the designers and makers of rugs: Pearl K. McGown, consultant to Sturbridge Corporation, Old Sturbridge Village Museum, Sturbridge, Massachusetts; Ruth Hall; Helen Fetzer; Betty Swezy; Daga Ramsey; Alice Kaufman; Minna Zaret; Sol Zaret; Professor Irwin Corey; Helen Tandler; Sandra Choron; Elizabeth Malament; Stephanie Goodstein; Florence Friedman; Charlotte Donaday; Lucia Fragiacomo; Mimi Waldhorn; Alice Epstein; Florence Smith; Dorothy Conrad; Monica Carl; Shulamith Miller; Kenneth Katz; Ellen Katz; Dubby Wassyng; Bernard Glickman; Shirley Glickman; Lynne Scire. Thanks also to Irma Philmus; Ken Philmus; Ruth Levine; Doris Berger; Gladys Blum; Alice Parsons; Marie O'Connell; and to Deborah Magid for her drawings.

INTRODUCTION

Today we live in a world of mass production. The craftsman of old has been put out of business by the growing demands of a culture more interested in quantity than quality. "Handmade" is seldom seen on labels, which usually boast of being made of synthetic materials. I am often reminded of the short story, "Quality," by John Galsworthy, in which an old shoemaker sadly retires because no one is interested in paying for his handmade shoes of fine quality. Today, few can afford the luxury of having clothing or furniture made by hand. I treasure my antique furniture that was made without benefit of factory machines and shows all the signs of tender loving care in its craftsmanship and finishing. Somehow, mass production tends to rob things of their individuality.

Men and women alike are developing a growing interest in craft hobbies, which are both decorative and functional. Rug making seems to be one of the most popular outlets for this desire to create something of one's own, because rugs serve a useful purpose and are always on display for you and your friends to admire. Making rugs can be either a family project or an individual effort. I feel guilty about "just" viewing television, so I always have some handwork project ready to work on. Also, meetings and long trips seem to move faster when my hands are busy. In addition, I find that rug making is easier on my eyes than close embroidery.

The cost of a rug can be controlled by the choice of material, the technique you select, and the size. However, don't plan on any handmade rugs being inexpensive. Unless you are prepared to use good quality yarns and canvas, I don't recommend that you make rugs. Too much time and effort is involved to use inferior materials that will never look good and will invariably wear poorly.

I have tried in this book to offer a wide variety of methods, designs, and materials. Eventually, you will find a favorite method, but try different techniques, and don't be afraid to let your personal whims and creativeness have their fling. These personal touches will give your rug its individuality.

Have fun and good luck!

1 HISTORY

The invention of the rug or carpet has been attributed to the Egyptians, the Chinese, the Mayas, and other early cultures. Perhaps each culture did invent its own version of what today we call a rug. Some say that the Chinese were the first to tie small knots or tufts onto the warp (vertical) threads of a loom to create a pile. Wherever rugs started, historians find evidence of them as far back as 2000 B.C. Preben Liebetrau, in his book, *Oriental Rugs in Colour*, recounts a fascinating story about an early rug:

> During excavations in a valley of the Altai range, South Siberia, in 1947–49, the Russian archaeologist S. J. Rudenko found a very well-preserved rug in a grave-mound belonging to a prince of Altai who lived in the fifth century B.C. Made of wool, a perishable substance, only chance has preserved this rug in such good condition. It would seem that the burial-mound had not long been raised when it was visited by grave-robbers. They removed metals and precious stones, but took no interest in carpets. Later on, torrents of water gushed in through the openings they made, and filled the burial-chamber. The water turned into ice, and this accident has given us a "deep-frozen" rug with its colours wonderfully preserved.

Rugs, like many other things, originated from necessity, and their creators made no attempt initially at being artistic. Nomadic tribes needed something to protect themselves from the cold earth floors of their tents. At first, animal hides were used. Indian tribles in North and South America, particularly the wandering Navajos and sheepherders, began to use the wool of their sheep for weaving blankets and rugs to keep themselves warm. These were softer and warmer than animal hides. They always traveled with their crude looms and made simple rugs in natural colors of black, brown, and white. Later, with the arrival of the Spaniards, the Indians became interested in color and eventually learned to make use of natural sources for dyes, such as berries, leaves, flowers, and roots.

The early colonists coming to America brought few home furnishings with them. Only the very rich could afford to send to Europe for supplies that usually included fine Oriental rugs. The poor colonists had little to brighten their homes, and the cold floors made rugs a necessity. They saved every scrap of used, worn material that was no longer serviceable for passing down or remaking into a coat, suit, or dress for the next in line in the family.

These worn scraps eventually became a braided or loomed rug. The only looms the colonists had were crude, small handmade ones. This meant that they had to weave the larger rugs in sections. Frances Lichten, in *Folk Art of Rural Pennsylvania,* says:

> Preparing and sewing rags was an occupation which took up many a winter evening. Discarded garments were brought out, cut or torn into strips about ½ inch wide and sewn together to be rolled later into balls. After a woman accumulated enough balls of rags, she discussed its production with the neighborhood carpet-weaver, an artisan whose trade was a common one at that time. . . . Material was also selected to be set aside for braided rugs, which were great favorites.

Braiding came naturally to these women whose long hair was usually kept neat by means of a braid or two. The rugs made from these scraps were sometimes the only bits of bright color in their homes.

Beautiful rugs continue to brighten our homes today as more and more people take up the ancient craft of rug making. Making a rug—whether of discarded remnants or raw wool—satisfies one's creative urges and at the same time provides one with an attractive and functional furnishing.

2 HOOKED RUGS

HISTORY

Most of us think of hooking as an American folk art. Actually, hooking has been traced to the Vikings, who, because of the cold temperatures, hooked thick furlike rugs. From the Scandinavians rug hooking spread to the British Isles, where, like many other crafts, it was brought to the American colonies by the settlers. Some of the most beautiful hooked rugs are American, made from used fabrics. These rugs represent a part of the folk heritage of our country which we have only lately begun to appreciate and cherish.

The earliest rugs were primitive in design, usually showing baskets, flowers, animals, and patriotic motifs. As the early settlers became more confident of their skills, they developed more and more unusual designs, which we still copy today. Many show the influence of the Oriental rugs that the seamen brought to the colonies from abroad.

Hooked rugs are practical, beautiful, and, if old fabrics are used, inexpensive to make. Many different effects can be achieved by varying pile heights and wool textures. An unlimited choice of patterns and designs makes hooking an exciting technique.

HOOKING METHODS

There are many ways to hook a rug. The traditional method is called hand hooking and uses a small crochet-type hook set in a pear-shaped wooden handle. Years ago the local blacksmith made the hook from a nail, which he filed and bent into shape. The tiny hook produces a fine loop and allows for intricate detail and color variation within a small area. It can handle strands of material as short as two inches and

FLAGS AND FLOWERS. Hooked rug. Rags hooked through burlap and left uncut for background. Flags and flowers are wool yarn. From *Country Life in America*, 1926. (See color plate 2.)

EARTH'S ENDOWMENT. Hooked rug designed by Pearl K. McGown and made by Charlotte Donaday.

MY REVERIE. Hooked rug designed by Pearl K. McGown and made by Charlotte Donaday.

CHICKENS IN A CIRCLE. Antique American hooked rag rug. Collection of James Abbe, Jr.

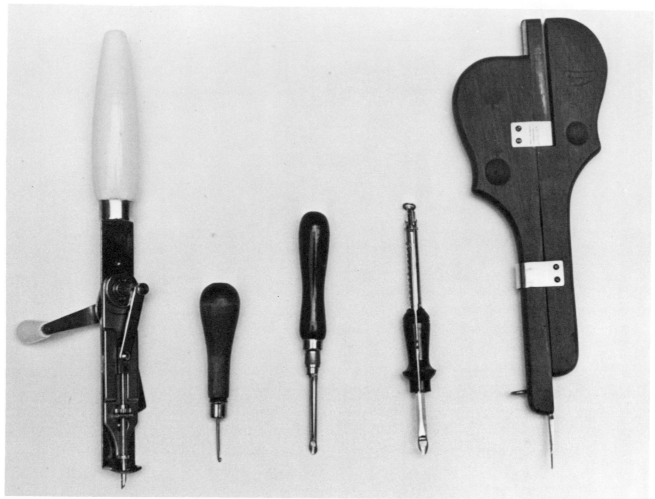

Hooking tools. From left to right: eggbeater, hand hook, punch hook, adjustable punch hook, shuttle hook.

needs no threading. The hand hook is most suitable for fabric strips. This method is probably the most difficult to master, as you must control the loop heights yourself.

A *punch hook* is a very popular tool for hooking, since it is faster and easier to handle than the hand hook. The height of the loops is automatically controlled by the punch hook. It is most suitable for use with yarn but can take cloth strips if they are cut evenly and narrow enough to slide through the hook easily.

The *shuttle hook,* like the punch hook, is a fast hooking tool, easy to use, and also very popular for hooking with yarn or cloth. It requires the use of both hands working together and is usually adjustable for loop height.

The *tappenalen,* a rather new type of hook, looks like an eggbeater and works like one. It moves as quickly as your hand can guide it. I find that it tends to run away from me, making it difficult to control. It is even faster than the punch or shuttle hook.

Foundation Fabric or Backing

Any evenly and firmly woven fabric is suitable for hooking, although it cannot be too dense or it will not accept the needle. Some people use burlap because it is inexpensive and easy to hook through. Ten-ounce burlap is easy to work on, but 12-ounce is preferable because it is firmer. Jute, of which burlap is made, is not as strong as cotton and linen. I prefer a monk's cloth or a rug warp cloth of a 2-ply weave which will wear better than burlap but costs more. Some backings have vertical and/or horizontal guidelines, which are helpful for transferring designs. If you use heavy yarn, select a looser weave than one you would use for lightweight yarn.

These fabrics come in widths up to 200 inches. When you figure yardage, allow for a 2-inch hem all around, plus a few extra inches for attaching to your frame and ½ inch for folding under to prevent raveling. If you need a wider width than is available, cut off selvages and overlap two pieces for about an inch, trying to match threads, and baste them together on both edges before you begin to hook. Hook across these seams rather than along them, going through both thicknesses. Work on a rectangular foundation regardless of the shape of the finished rug so that it will be easy to attach to the frame without distortion.

If I plan to use a punch hook, I rub the backing with ordinary paraffin, which leaves a light film of wax and makes punching much easier.

Monk's cloth with guidelines

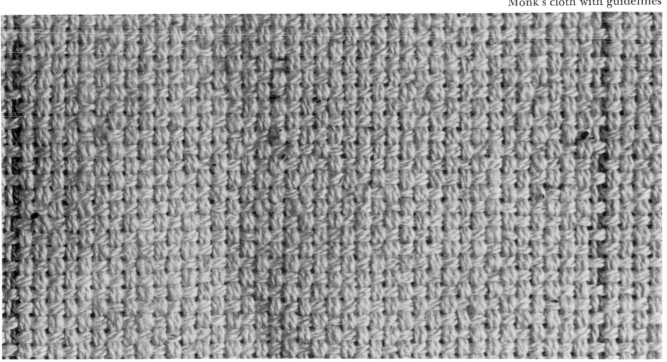

Piles

You can hook with either cut fabric or yarn. If you choose to use old fabrics, you can follow the instructions for preparation in the chapter on braiding. Be sure that you have enough of your background color before you start using old fabrics. If you want to dye used fabrics, see the chapter on dyeing. New fabrics simply require cutting. There are mechanical cutting machines that will cut 6 strips at one time. Some have changeable cutting blades so that the same cutter can be used for cutting wider strips for braiding. Of course you can always cut the fabric by hand. It takes much more time, but the unevenness of hand-cut fabric lends a certain charming quality to the finished rug. Our ancestors always cut by hand.

I prefer to use all-wool fabrics because they wear well and look lovely. Flannel may also be used because it doesn't fray, but a rug made of all flannel sometimes has a store-bought look. Try combining flannel with tweeds and textured fabrics. Tweeds should be cut on the straight of the fabric or they will fray easily.

Knitted fabric tends to become matted, and it is not advisable to use it in large areas. If you are using knitted fabrics in the same rug with flannel or tweed, cut the knitted strips slightly wider, making certain that you do not cut on the bias but with the weave of the fabric. Pull each strip to stretch it out before you start to hook with it.

If you use mixtures of wool and synthetics, try to find those that have a large percentage of wool. Whatever you use, make certain it is durable.

Mechanical cutting machine used for cutting strips of fabric

If you wash your new fabrics (as you do the used fabrics) or home-dye them, your rug will also be washable and colorfast.

The width of the fabric strips depends on the weight of the fabric and your own feeling about hooking. Generally, you would use finer strips for detailing and design than for background. The old primitive rugs we see in museums and antique shops have wide strips and rather large loops. Experiment on a sample before you begin to cut all your fabric. Try flannel at $\frac{1}{2}$ inch, medium-weight fabric at $\frac{1}{4}$ inch, and heavy wools at $\frac{1}{8}$ inch. If you have difficulty pulling the material through the foundation fabric, try making the strips narrower.

If you prefer to hook with yarn, you will save time, as you eliminate the preparation and cutting necessary with fabric, but you won't save money. Yarn is expensive, especially a good quality wool yarn. Some supply shops have a natural yarn that you can dye yourself. If you are particular about colors, you will enjoy the results of home dyeing.

To save money, you might try unraveling old sweaters and using the yarn in double or triple strands. I don't advise doing a whole rug with used sweater yarn, but combined with heavier rug yarn, it will certainly hold its own.

Quantities

It is difficult to estimate the quantities of fabric you will need, as they are dependent on many factors (width, size of loop, backing fabric, etc.). I suggest that you make sure before you start that your fabric is easily available. Sometimes, doing a sample square with a measured quantity will give you some idea. Approximately $\frac{1}{2}$ pound should cover a square foot.

Yarn is easier to figure. Eight to 10 ounces of rug yarn covers about a 12-inch square. Always overestimate. Rug yarn is often returnable if you make prior arrangements with your supply shop.

Frames

Hooked rugs are made on a frame, enabling the backing fabric to be stretched tightly and at the same time freeing both hands for hooking. The frame itself can be as simple as a wooden picture frame or an artist's canvas stretcher. If you want to make one yourself, use narrow lightwood slats about 2 inches wide and 1 inch thick which are strong enough to resist some pulling. Make a rectangle of any size convenient for you to handle and reinforce the corners with metal braces screwed to wood. The size of the frame does not dictate the size of the rug. As you finish a section of the rug, you remove it from the frame and move another section of the foundation onto the frame.

If you prefer, you can also make a larger frame on a stand. They are available ready-made in sizes ranging from 20 inches to 60 inches.

Rug mounted on simple wooden frame
used for hooking. Rug designed and made
by Lucia Fragiacomo.

Large frame on wheels that is used for
hooking in a standing position. Rug designed
and made by Mimi Waldhorn.

These usually have adjustable tilting devices. There are also frames and hoops that are worked at your lap. Most rug-making supply firms stock hooking frames.

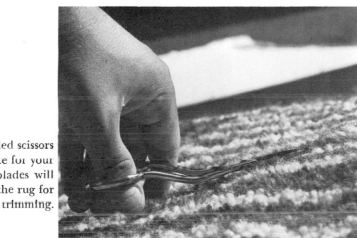

Frame on a stand

Scissors

Special scissors are made for rug making. They have bent handles that allow space for your fingers and yet will lie flat against the rug for trimming. If you have shears at home, they will serve the purpose as long as they are sharp. Dull scissors will fray your yarn or fabric.

Bent-handled scissors allow space for your fingers, yet the blades will be flat against the rug for trimming.

PREPARING FOUNDATION FABRICS OR BACKINGS

Cut the foundation 2 inches larger on all sides than your finished rug to allow for a hem and tacking to frame. Fold over ½ inch of the outer edge where you tack. Pull or draw a thread from the length and width of your foundation fabric. This will give you a straight line that acts as a cutting guide.

Define the size of your rug by outlining it with an indelible pen.

If fabric ravels easily, such as in the case of burlap, turn back ½ inch and hem.

With a yardstick find the center of the backing by drawing lines across the width and length. Your fabric is now divided into four quarters. This will be helpful when you apply the design.

CREATING YOUR OWN DESIGNS

In addition to the designs I have graphed in this book, there are many ways you can create your own designs, even if you are not an artist. Some of the most beautiful hooked rugs are the ones done by our ancestors using primitive designs of nonartists.

A simple but lovely design is one with a few solid borders of varying widths and different colors. The main pattern can be a repeated design scattered here and there on a solid or mottled background. Almost any shape that you fancy can be repeated—a circle, a star, a pretty leaf. Usually you can find something around the house to use as a pattern to trace onto the backing.

Another method of designing your rug is to fold heavy paper the size of your rug (not the foundation size, which was cut larger to fit onto the frame) in half, then in half again, then in half again. Cut odd shapes here and there along edges of folds. (I'm sure you have all done this as children.) When you open the paper, you will have an interesting pattern that you can trace onto the backing. If you want borders, start with a smaller piece of paper and center the paper when you start tracing, leaving room for as many borders as you would like.

Geometrics are always in good taste and are traditional Americana. A plain "hit-or-miss" pattern (making use of any odd bits of yarn or fabric you have around the house and using it in rows of haphazard color) is subtle and won't clash with other prints in your room. These rugs can be done in blocks outlined with a dark color and bordered with solid rows, or you can use the hit-or-miss throughout the entire rug. Small blocks done diagonally in hit-or-miss were popular with the colonists. I saw a beautiful one in a museum which was composed of tan and brown blocks with wavy stripes of reds, blues, and pale beige. The dark blues and reds were used in one corner, gradually working up to the palest colors. If you are doing a narrow rug or runner, try having stripes that go across the width. It will create the illusion of a wider rug. A lovely border can be created with hit-or-miss hooking. Decide on the width of your border. Then do horizontal rows of many colors until you have a square. Then reverse your direction and do vertical rows of the same size.

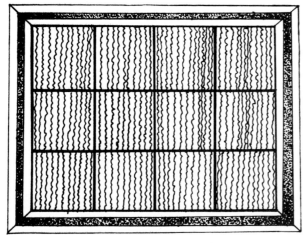

Hit-or-miss in blocks

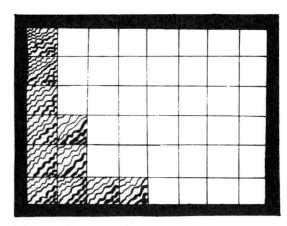

Diagonal hit-or-miss in small blocks

Another traditional border, known by three names depending on the area, is the lamb's tongue or fish scale or oyster shell. See page 92 and color plate 20 for a whole rug done in this design.

A series of plain shaded borders helps to highlight an interesting center design.

Try a French curve (available at any stationers) to make a border of vines to which you can add simple leaves and possibly a flower here and there.

If you want to make a stair runner, you can make a simple hit-or-miss for the stair tread and a design for the riser. If you do it in one piece, be very careful to measure your stairs exactly so that your design will be in the proper place on each riser.

Avoid intricate details in hooking, as the loops do not really define tiny things and they will be lost. Keep your background simple if your design is a busy one.

Don't be afraid to experiment on your foundation. Use a pencil first which can be erased or gone over easily. When you are satisfied with your plan, use an indelible pen to go over your design.

Hit-or-miss runner

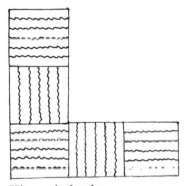

Hit-or-miss border

Lamb's tongue border

Vine, leaf, and flower border

27

TRANSFERRING DESIGNS

There are many ways to transfer a design onto the backing fabric.

Shapes can be cut out of stiff cardboard and placed on the backing, then traced with an indelible pen. Many things you have around the house can be used to trace a design on the backing, such as dishes of various sizes, books, bricks, oval bowls, oak or maple leaves, etc. The advantage of using this method is that you can arrange and rearrange the design until it pleases your fancy.

Another method of transferring a design is to trace a drawing or picture over dressmaker's carbon paper onto the backing. Make sure the carbon paper is face down on the foundation. You can tape many sheets of carbon paper together to make one large sheet so that you can do the whole rug at once.

To enlarge and transfer a design, you can use the box or grid method. Rule squares of equal size over the entire design. Then rule the same number of squares on a sheet of thin paper the actual size of your rug. These will be much larger boxes if the size of your rug is larger than the original design. Now copy freehand each small box onto the larger equivalent box. You will be surprised at the accuracy of your enlargement. If a square is too complicated to copy freehand, divide that particular square into smaller squares and proceed to work freehand on these smaller sections.

Use a special indelible copying or transfer pencil (which will transfer the design to the backing when heat is applied) to draw the enlarged design onto the paper. Any art or rug supply shop has this transfer pencil. Pin the paper carefully to your rug backing with the pencilled side down, facing the fabric. Iron slowly until a test corner shows that your pattern has been transferred. Then continue to transfer the rest of your design.

Of course, if you are at all artistic, you can draw directly on the backing. Start with a light pencil sketch, and when you are satisfied with the design, go over it with an indelible pen. Be sure that the backing is taut when you work.

ATTACHING TO FRAME

For attaching the foundation to the frame, use extra-long thumbtacks, beginning at a corner and tacking along one width and length as far as you can go, then on the other width and length, pulling the fabric as taut as possible. Remember to keep fabric straight so the edges will be square. When you are ready to remove tacks to change to a new section of your rug, use a tack-puller or screwdriver.

Another method frequently used to attach foundation to frame is sewing it. Use heavy cord and a darning needle. Wrap the cord around the frame, then pull it through the edges of the foundation fabric, starting at the shorter end. Make sure your fabric is straight and taut. When you change the position of the fabric on the frame, let the finished section hang down on the far side of the frame away from your body and the unworked fabric hang down toward your lap.

If you use a frame on a stand, be sure to adjust it to a height that will enable you to sit comfortably. Use a straight-backed chair and sit way back in it, leaning forward from your waist rather than curling your shoulders down. This will prevent you from getting a backache. Make certain that you have good light when you work. Save your dark color areas for daylight.

HOOKING PROCEDURES

Hand hooks

The first thing to remember is that you will be working on the right side of the rug. The loops will be brought from underneath up to the top with the hook.

Hold the hook as you would a pencil, or, if it is more comfortable, hold the wooden handle in the palm of your right hand with your index finger on the steel shank about halfway down. With the hook facing the direction you are going, push through to the underside. Place your left hand underneath to guide the strip of fabric, which is held lightly between the thumb and the forefinger of your left hand, onto the hook. As your right hand pulls up the hook with the fabric wound on it to make a loop, press the shank against the foundation to enlarge the opening as much as possible, allowing more room for the fabric to come through. The first stitch of each strip won't be a loop; it will be the end piece, which is brought up from the bottom to the top and clipped to proper loop height later. Keep all cut ends on the right side of the rug, where they will blend in with the loops. If they are left on the back of the rug, they might accidentally get pulled, at which point the rest of the strip will pull out. When they are on the right side, the thickness of the pile will keep them in place. Skip one or two meshes of the foundation after each stitch and push the hook down again to pull up a loop. With some practice you will learn to regulate your loops so they are all the same height.

The height of the loop depends on your own need. A good loop height is 1/4 to 3/8 of an inch. For special effects, you can vary the loop heights. If you want to clip the loops, make them slightly higher. If

Hand hook

Guide yarn or fabric with your left hand while working the hook with your right hand.

29

you have pulled a loop up too high, use your left hand underneath to pull it back down slightly until it is the proper height. Don't take the hook out of the loop until it is the proper height. To release the hook, give it a slight twist and withdraw. You will soon develop a rhythm to your work which will help the procedure to go smoothly and efficiently.

If you find that in the process of making a loop you are pulling out the previous loop, relax your left-hand grasp of the fabric strip a little. It is probably not loose enough.

When you have finished a strip (they may be any length for hand hooking), bring the end up to the top and clip it to match the height of the other loops. Start the next strip by putting the hook in the same hole as the last end and bringing the new end up through the same hole.

When you start a new row, begin by leaving only one mesh bare between the rows. Avoid making the loops of the new row directly below the previous row. If you alternate them, your rug will look fuller. Don't try to crowd too many loops into an area, but don't leave bare spots either. Check on the back side to make sure there are no empty spaces. If you find a stitch that crosses over another stitch, clip it and bring both ends up to the right side. Always avoid crossovers.

It is a good idea to cut a few strips and hook with them before you cut any quantity, as you might find that they are too wide or too narrow.

When you have finished hooking and find that some loops are too high, you can clip them to the proper height. Clipping large areas gives a velvety appearance, although early New England rugs were rarely clipped.

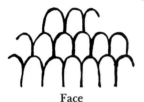

Alternate rows of hooking

Face

Back

Punch Hooks

With a punch hook you work from the underside of your rug and punch down to what will be the surface of the rug.

Most hooks come with two size punch needles. The large one can take one strand of heavy yarn or two strands of medium yarn or two or three strands of fine yarn. Just make sure that the yarn you select slides freely through the tube and eye of the needle.

The size of the loop on most hooks is adjustable. You can go from a loop of about 1/4 of an inch to one of 3/4 of an inch.

To thread the needle, hold the slotted side toward you, thread yarn through the ring from the outside, and then through the point from the inside. Pull about a foot of yarn through the point.

Now you will have to get the yarn through the slot. Hold on to the foot of yarn at the point end with your left hand. With your right hand pull the yarn until it slides into the slot. If it does not go in easily, the yarn might be too thick for the needle. Now you can pull

Simple punch hook

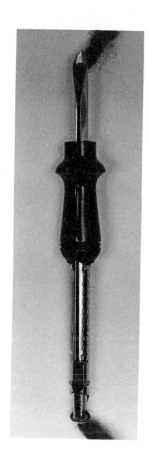

Adjustable punch hook

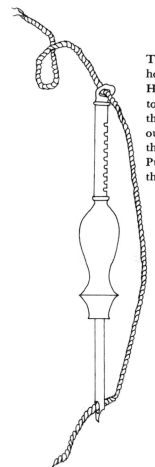

Threading the punch
hook:
Hold the slotted side
toward you, thread yarn
through the ring from the
outside, and then through
the point from the inside.
Pull about a foot of yarn
through the point.

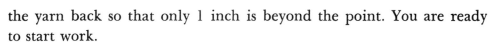

the yarn back so that only 1 inch is beyond the point. You are ready
to start work.

Sit so that you are higher than your frame. Make sure that your
yarn will flow freely or else it will be difficult to hook even loops. Keep
a good portion unwound as you work.

Hold the punch hook between your thumb and forefinger in an
upright position with the open side facing the direction in which you
will be going. If you change direction, turn the open side accordingly.
Let your hand rest on the backing. Twist your hand and punch the

Hold on to the foot
of yarn at the point end
with your left hand. With
your right hand pull the
yarn until it slides into
the slot.

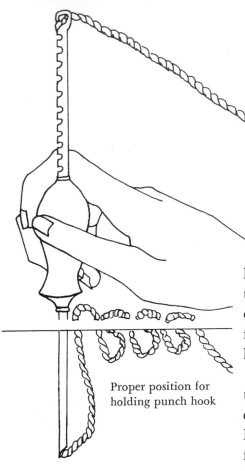

Proper position for
holding punch hook

hook down as far as it will go. Make certain that the handle is hitting
the backing. Without lifting your hand from the backing, pull the hook
out. Don't lift it higher than the backing—it should just clear the surface—and slide it to the next stitch and punch again. If you lift the
hook too high, you will be pulling the loop you just completed.

All your yarn ends—beginnings, too—should be pushed down to
the right side. The back, the side you are working on, should have no
ends and no stitches crossing over other ones. You can trim these ends
later. When you want to end a color, in order to prevent the last loop
from pulling out, hold onto it with your left hand as you withdraw
the threaded needle. Cut the yarn about 1 inch above the backing and
push it down to the front.

When you work, try to keep the same number of stitches to the
inch. The denser your loops, the better your rug will wear. For a
½-inch loop a good average is 4 stitches to the inch. Remember that
you should use short loops for designs that have a great deal of detail;
try to work about 6 rows in an inch.

Shuttle Hooks

Like the punch hook, the shuttle hook is worked from the back of
the rug.

Threading is simple. The yarn goes through the side loop and
down and through the eye of the needle from the loop side.

Shuttle hook

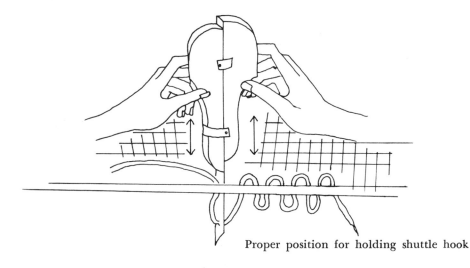

Proper position for holding shuttle hook

Plate 1

FLOWER POTS. Antique American hooked rug. Collection of Mr. and Mrs. Sol Zaret.

Plate 2

FLAGS AND FLOWERS. Antique American hooked rug.

Plate 3

LITTLE EASTLAND. Hooked rug designed by Pearl K. McGown and made by Helen Ernest. Instructions, pages 34–35.

Plate 4

LOG CABIN. Hooked rug designed by Pearl K. McGown and made by Helen Ernest. This design was inspired by the old favorite quilt design of the same name. Graph, page 53.

Plate 5

SIGNALS. Antique American hooked rug. Author's collection. Graph, page 41.

Plate 6

LOIS. Antique American hooked rug. Collection of Mr. and Mrs. Norman Schneyer.
Graph, page 51.

Page 7

INTERLOCKING "Y". Antique American hooked rug. Author's collection. Graph, page 43.

Page 8

JOSHUA. Antique American hooked rug. Collection of Mr. and Mrs. Sol Zaret. Graph, page 57.

Plate 9

DOUBLE CORNUCOPIA. Hooked rug designed by Ruth
Hall and made by Alice Persons.

Plate 10

PERUVIAN FOLK ART. Hooked rug designed by Pearl
K. McGown and made by Marie O'Connell.

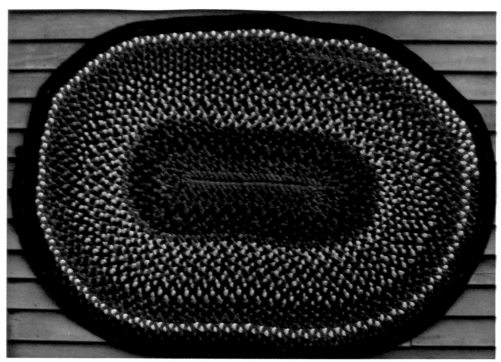

Plate 11

WILLIAM'S RUG. Braided rug designed and made by Helen Evola Fetzer. Instructions,
pages 61–69.

Plate 12

MOLLY. Antique braided oval rug. Author's collection. Instructions, pages 61–69.

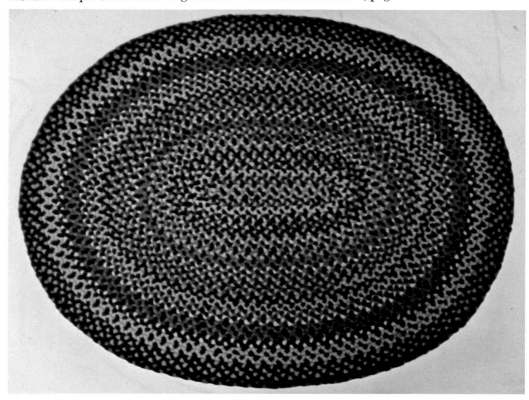

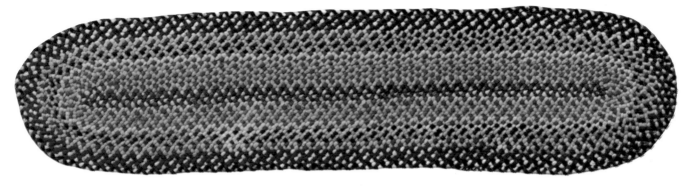

Plate 13

LONG TALL SALLY. Braided runner designed and made by Betty Swezey. Instructions, pages 61–69.

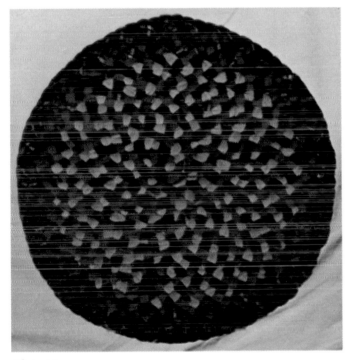

Plate 14

GUESSING GAMES. Antique braided chair pad. The manner in which the braids were laced together has puzzled many experts. Collection of James Abbe, Jr.

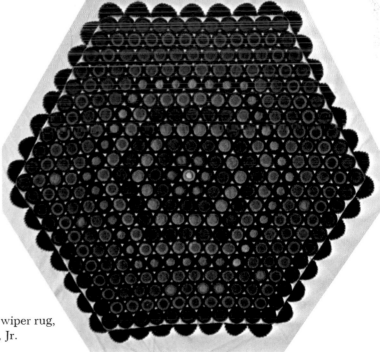

Plate 15

HEXAGON. New England antique pen wiper rug, circa 1880. Collection of James Abbe, Jr. Instructions, page 77.

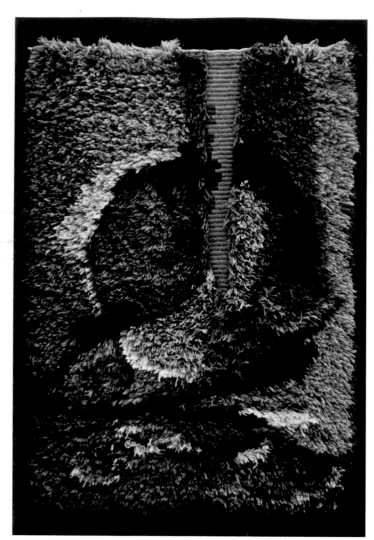

Plate 16

VISBY. Rya and flat seam combined. Designed and made by Daga Ramsey.

Plate 17

HAVAMAL. Rya and flat seam combined. Designed and made by Daga Ramsey.

Plate 18

Latch hook rug inspired by Fernand Léger's "Three Musicians." Designed and made by Alice Kaufman.

Plate 19

Latch hook rug inspired by Pablo Picasso's "Young Woman with a Looking Glass." Designed and made by Alice Kaufman.

Plate 20

SHEEP. Latch hook rug designed and made by Minna Zaret. Instructions, page 97.

Plate 21

FRAN. Latch hook rug designed and made by Professor Irwin Corey. Graph, page 101.

Plate 23

RUNNING BROOK. Needlepoint rug inspired by Navajo motif using continental stitch. Designed and made by author. Graph, page 115.

Plate 24

PRAYER RUG. Needlepoint rug using continental stitch. Designed by author and made by Helen Tandler. Graph, page 117.

Plate 22

CUBES WITH DOGS. Needlepoint rug using basketweave, continental, and cross stitches. Designed and made by author. Graph, page 135.

Plate 25

BOKARA. Needlepoint rug using continental and basketweave stitches. Designed by author and made by Helen Tandler. Graph, page 137.

Plate 26

HARRY. Needlepoint rug using basketweave and continental stitches. Designed by author and made by Sandra Choron. Graph, page 119.

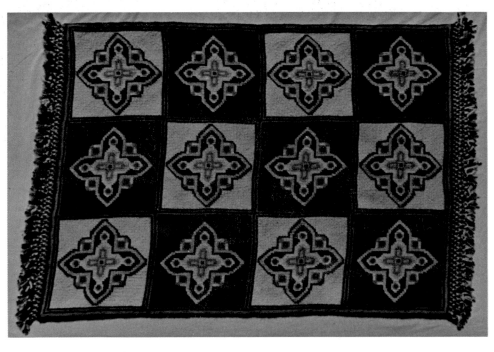

Plate 27

STEPPING STONES. Antique needlepoint rug (unfinished), using soumak stitch.
Collection of Eunice Plesser. Graph, page 127.

Plate 28

ORIENTAL BAZAAR. Needlepoint rug using continental and basketweave stitches. Designed by Sol Zaret and made by Minna Zaret. Graphs, pages 123–125.

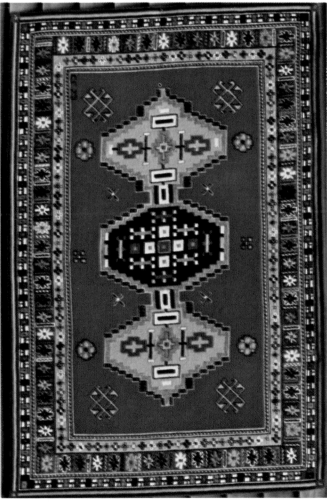

Plate 29

PERSIAN DELIGHT. Needlepoint rug using continental and basketweave stitches inspired cover design for author's *The Needlepoint Workbook of Traditional Designs.* Designed and made by author. Graphs, pages 129–131.

Plate 30

OHIO OVAL. Crocheted rug designed and made by Elizabeth Malament. Instructions, pages 144–145.

Plate 31

LONDON SQUARES. Crocheted rug designed and made by Elizabeth Malament. Instructions, page 147.

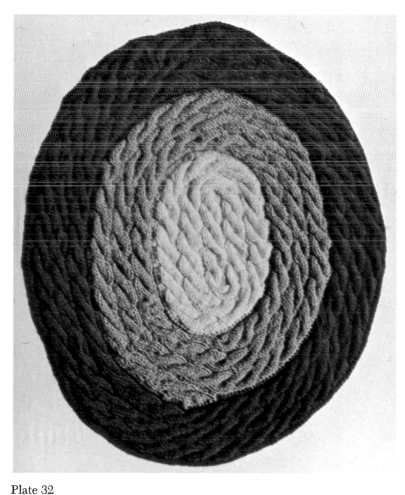

Plate 32

STEPHANIE. Knitted rug designed by Elizabeth Malament and made by Stephanie Goodstein. Instructions, page 173.

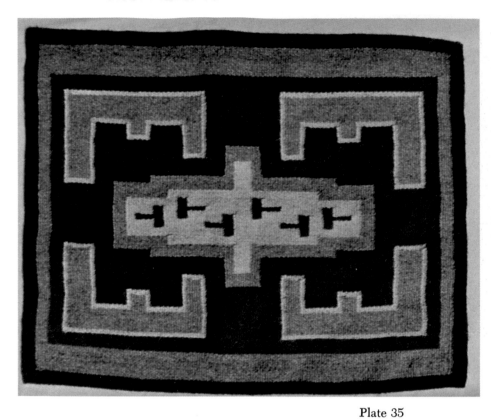

Plate 33

JACK'S RUG. Woven rug designed and made by Florence Friedman. Graph, page 187.

Plate 34

DOUBLE ARROW. Woven rug designed and made by Florence Friedman. Graph, page 189.

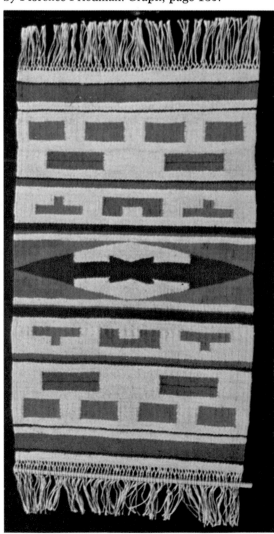

Plate 35

ANIMAL CRACKERS. Woven Polish wall hanging. Author's collection. Graph, page 191.

Both hands are used to shift the wooden sections up and down. As you lower the right section, the needle goes through the backing. As you raise it, the left section lowers to secure the loop. The shuttle will move automatically to the next position, and you are ready to repeat the procedure.

Some shuttle hooks are not adjustable for different loop heights. Some come with three or four adjustments and two sets of points to accommodate yarn and fabric strips.

Eggbeater Hooks

This fast hooking tool, which is called *tappenalen* in its native Denmark, moves automatically as you work and can do up to 500 loops a minute. It is adjustable for loop height. Threading is difficult and time-consuming. Complete instructions come with the hook. On the rare occasions when I do use the "eggbeater," I thread the yarn through a needle and then follow the directions, pushing through the various holes with the threaded needle. This imported Danish hooking tool is made to use with 4-ply knitting yarns rather than the heavier rug yarns. You might consider this a drawback. The speed with which you can work is the eggbeater's main asset.

Eggbeater hook

WHERE TO START

Always work from right to left when you are working horizontally. If you are hooking a vertical line, work up or down, whichever is easier.

Start by outlining the pattern first. Follow the contour of the design for a few rows, then fill in with either curves or swirls, working toward the center.

Do your borders next. Since edges of rugs get the most wear, hook rows and stitches closer together for the outermost two or three rows. If you are using fabric, save a strong material for the edges. Also, never end a row at a corner. It will weaken your edge. Work around each corner for several stitches before starting another strip.

When you are ready to fill in your background, hook the first rows close to the outline of the design, then fill in the rest.

Directional Hooking

There are many ways to hook the background. Some people like to mix and blend various colors. You can work in short curving lines, diagonal lines, swirls or half-moons, or just plain horizontal or vertical rows. You will get different effects in the background by directional hooking. See "The Hobbit," page 59. With practice you can use your imagination freely. If you plan to cut your loops, the direction you hook in will be of little consequence.

Checking

Before you remove the rug from the frame, check the back and edges to make sure that there are no thin places. If you find any, fill them in without splitting the loops you have already done and without crossing over existing rows.

Ripping

Don't leave something in your rug that you are unhappy about. If you are in doubt about something, place the rug on the floor and look at it from that perspective. Then, if you still want to rip it out, use tweezers to pull out the loops carefully. Try to find an end, push it down through the backing, then pull gently, and you should have no trouble. Fill in any spaces you have ripped out.

DESIGNS

LITTLE EASTLAND

LITTLE EASTLAND. Hooked rug designed by Pearl K. McGown and made by Helen Ernest. (See color plate 3)

To copy this fascinating rug, trace the four diamonds first. (Use stiff cardboard cut to shape for tracing.) Then do freehand lines around them as shown in the photograph. If your lines are not exactly the

same as the ones in the photo, don't worry. Your rug will be just as interesting. The border repeats the smallest size diamond. Use a dark color for your outlines (navy, black, brown) and fill in with shaded tones of various colors. For example, if you use blue, use 4 or 5 tones of blue between two dark lines.

SUNBURST

To make this exciting rug, draw a circle on your backing fabric any size you desire. With a yardstick, starting from the center, mark lines from the center of the circle down to the edge. These stripes may be of different widths. As you hook each section, start with the palest yellow (almost white) and work out to the edge, using a darker color each time you change colors. Don't end colors at the same place in each band. Use off-white, pale yellows, light oranges, rusts, and browns.

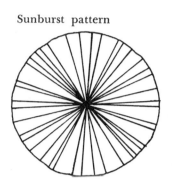
Sunburst pattern

SUNBURST. Hooked rug designed and made by Alice Epstein.

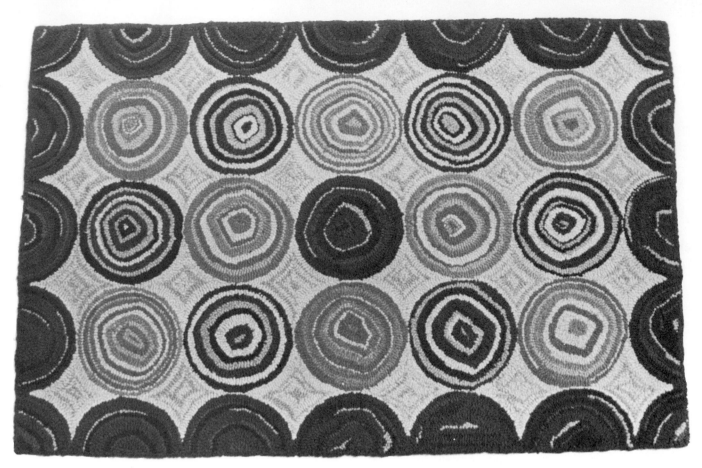

CARELESS CIRCLES. Hooked
rug designed and made by
Minna Zaret.

CARELESS CIRCLES

This rug is really simple to copy. Use a round dish (a dinner plate
will do) to trace circles on your backing. Place the circles as shown,
or in any other place your fancy leads you. Start hooking by outlining
each large circle, then fill in by doing one or two rounds of each color.
As you see, your circles do not have to be perfect; in fact, they shouldn't
look like an engineer did them. Put a diamond (again, not a perfectly
shaped one) in each space. This rug was hooked in shades of warm
golds and reds. Any colors you choose will enhance this charming
design.

MANHASSET—STAIR RUNNER AND MATCHING RUG

Some imagination and household articles made this pattern an
easy one to trace. First, decide on the size of your project. For the stair
runner, work in at least three different sections. Divide your backing
fabric into rectangles of equal size. Use a glass to trace the small circles.
Notice the different ways the three circle combinations on the rug are
filled in. Use a plate for the larger circles. A ruler is used to mark the
triangles. The teardrop shapes were traced from a large ashtray. You
can use any odd-shaped thing you have around the house. The borders
are mottled with colors used in the rug.

MANHASSET. Hooked stair runner and matching
rug designed and made by Alice Epstein.

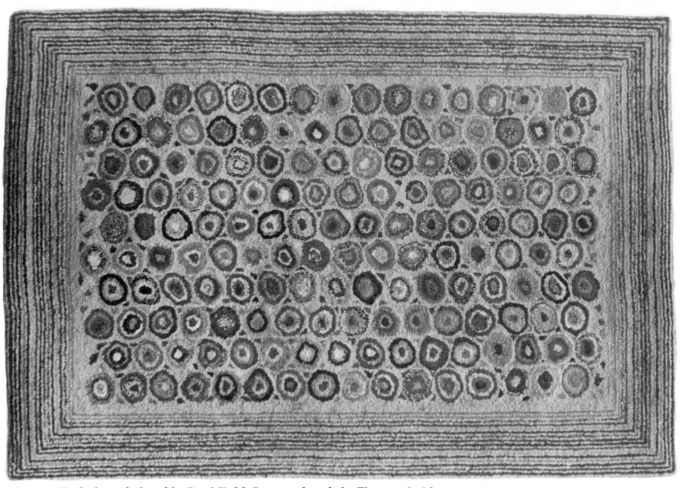

CAT'S PAW. Hooked rug designed by Pearl K. McGown and made by Florence Smith.

JIMMY'S HIT-OR-MISS. Antique American hooked rug. Collection of James Abbe, Jr.

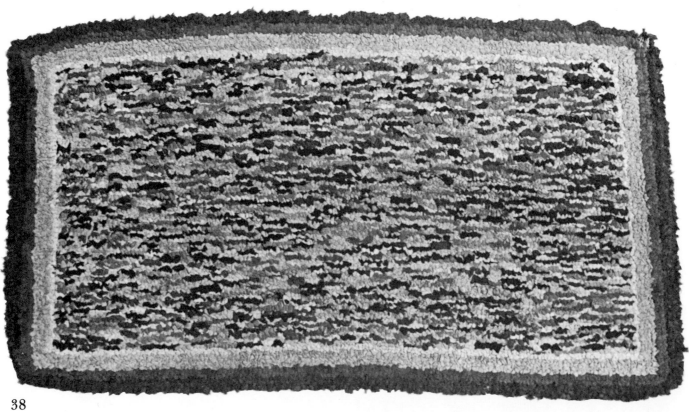

CAT'S PAW

This rug is similar to Careless Circles, page 36, except that much smaller circles are used and straight rows are repeated in different colors for the border. Cat's Paw is an excellent way to use up odds and ends of leftover yarn or fabric.

JIMMY'S HIT-OR-MISS

This American antique rug is charming in its simplicity. Rows of hit-or-miss (random color hooking) are enclosed by solid borders.

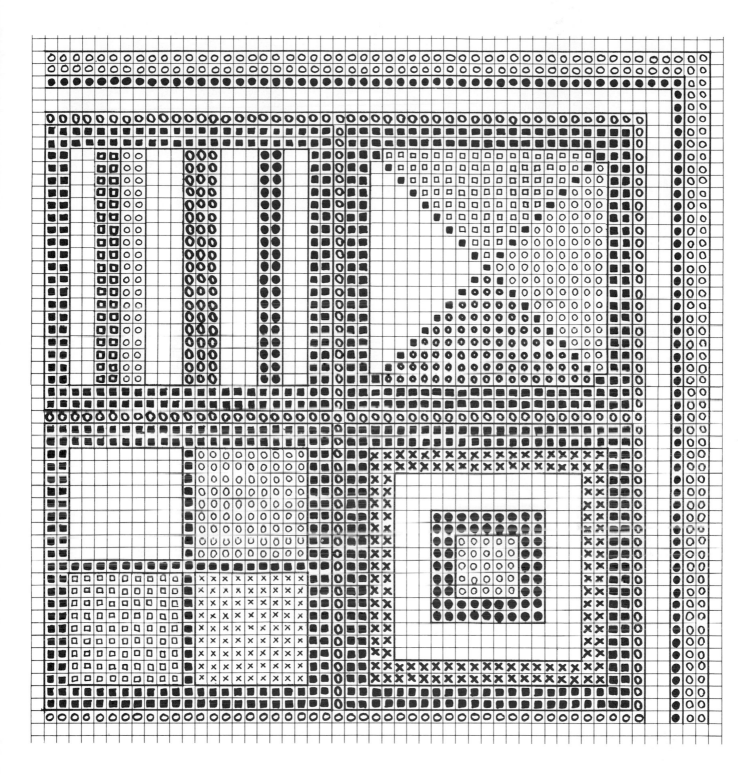

SIGNALS. Antique American hooked rug. Author's collection. (See color plate 5)

42

INTERLOCKING "Y." Antique American hooked rug. Author's collection. (See color plate 7)

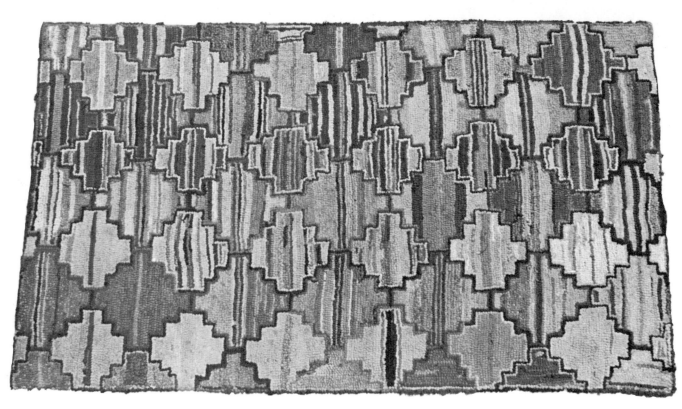

CAMDEN LIGHTS. Antique American hooked rug. Collection of James Abbe, Jr.

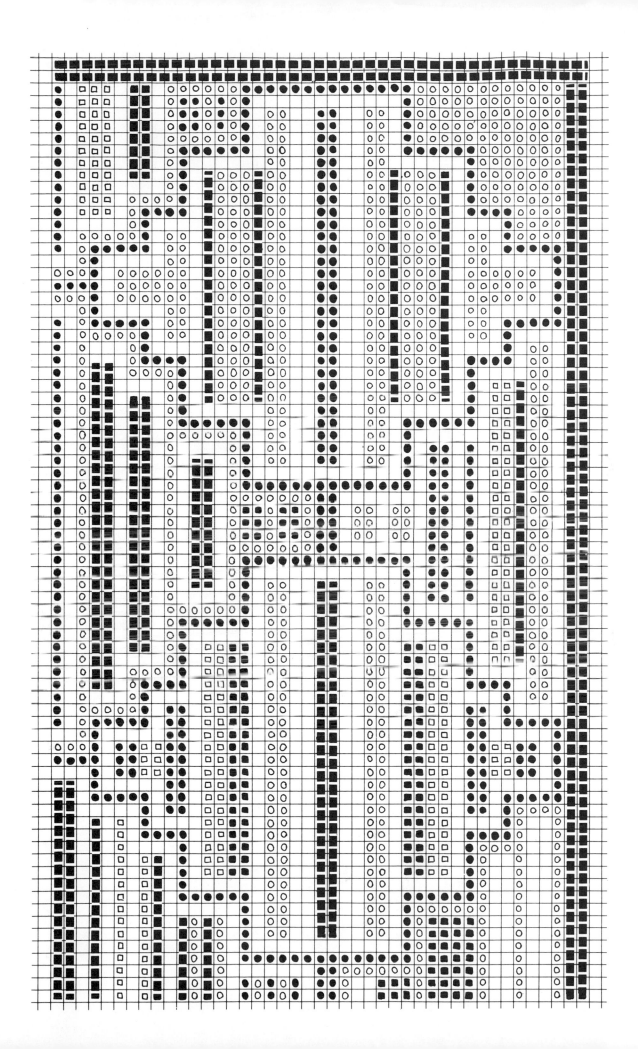

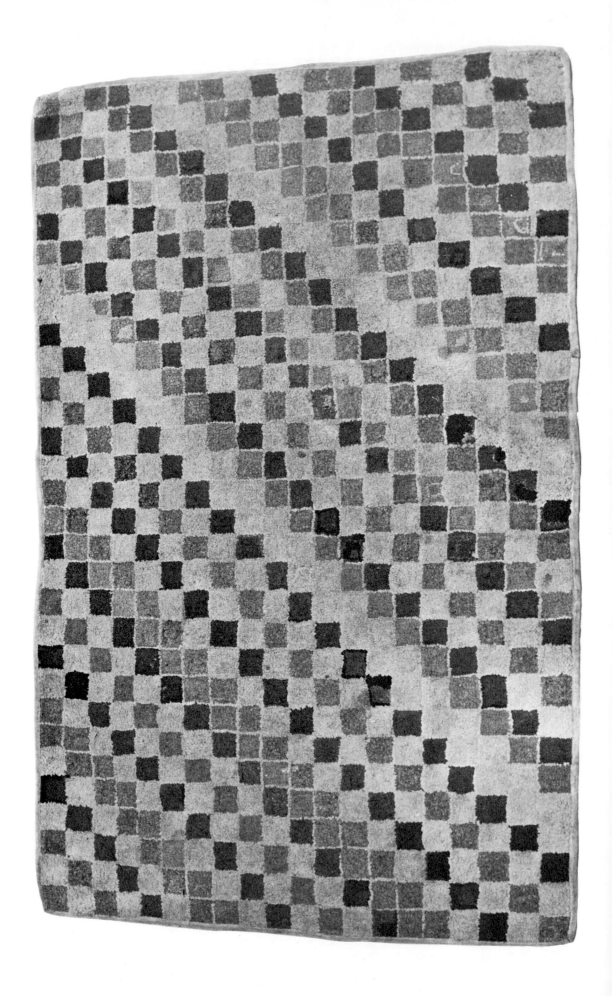

46

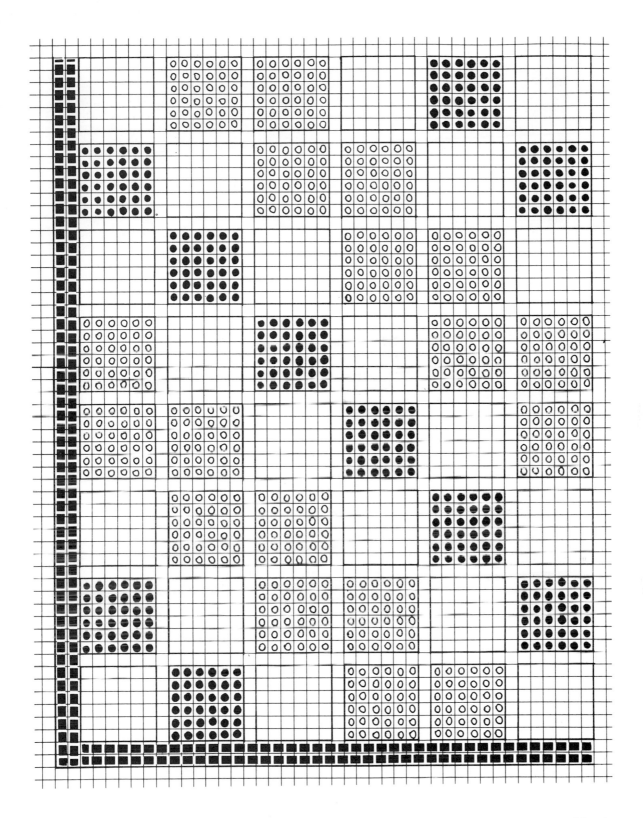

DIAGONAL CHECKERS. Antique American hooked rug. The design is suitable for latch hooked and embroidered rugs. Collection of James Abbe, Jr.

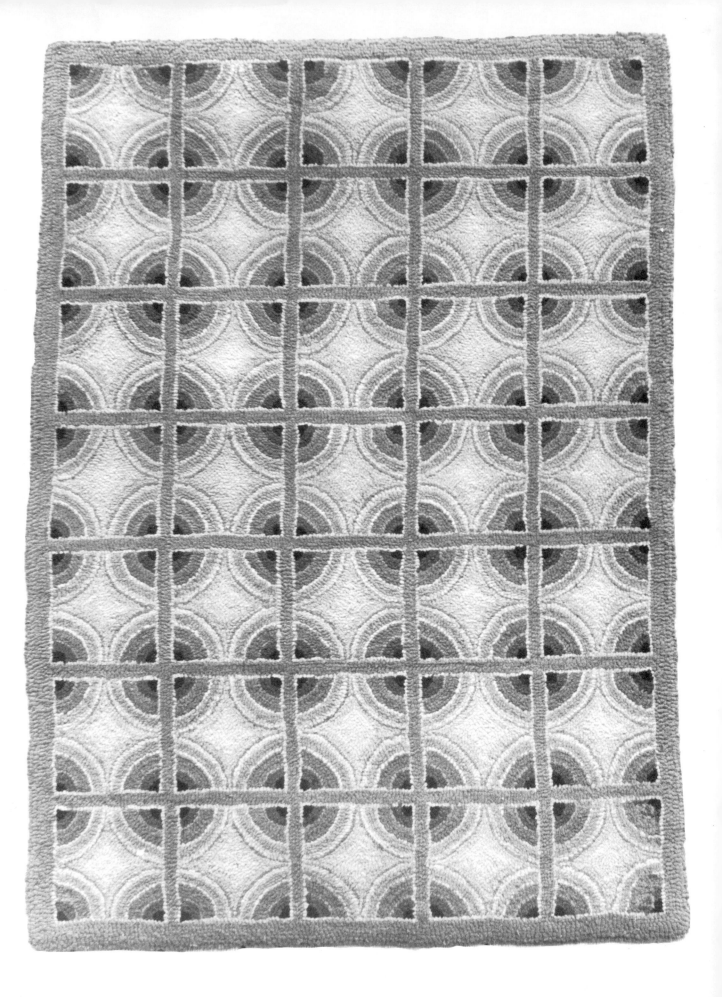

48

LITTLE GEOMETRICS. Hooked rug designed by Pearl K. McGown and made by Dorothy Conrad.

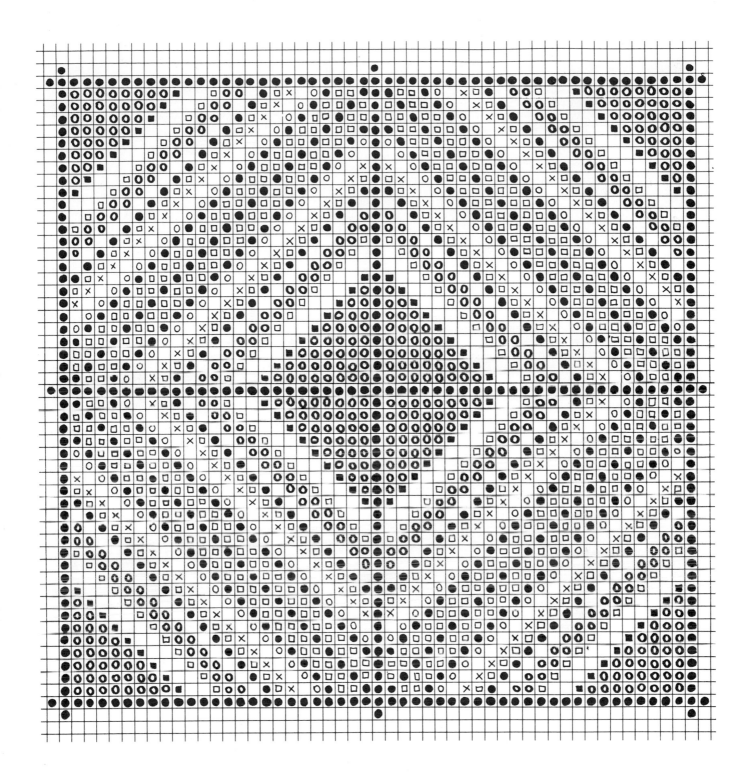

LOIS. Section of antique American hooked rug. Collection of Mr. and Mrs. Norman Schneyer. (See color plate 6)

52

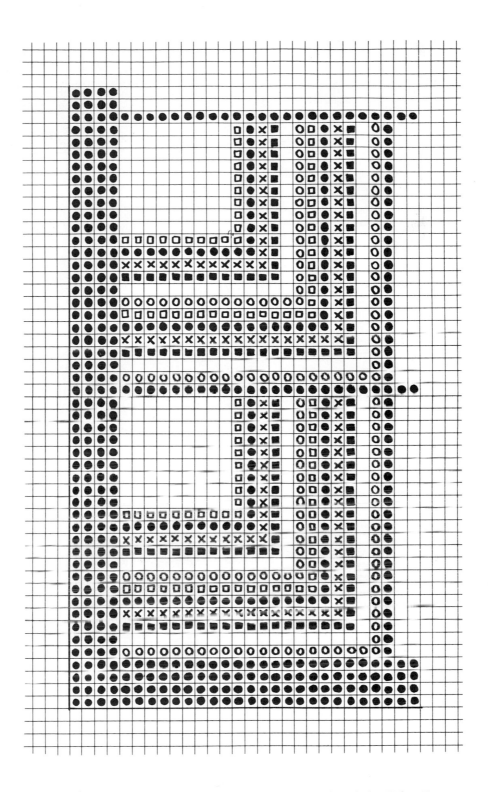

LOG CABIN. Hooked rug designed by Pearl K. McGown and made by Helen Ernest. (See color plate 4)

54

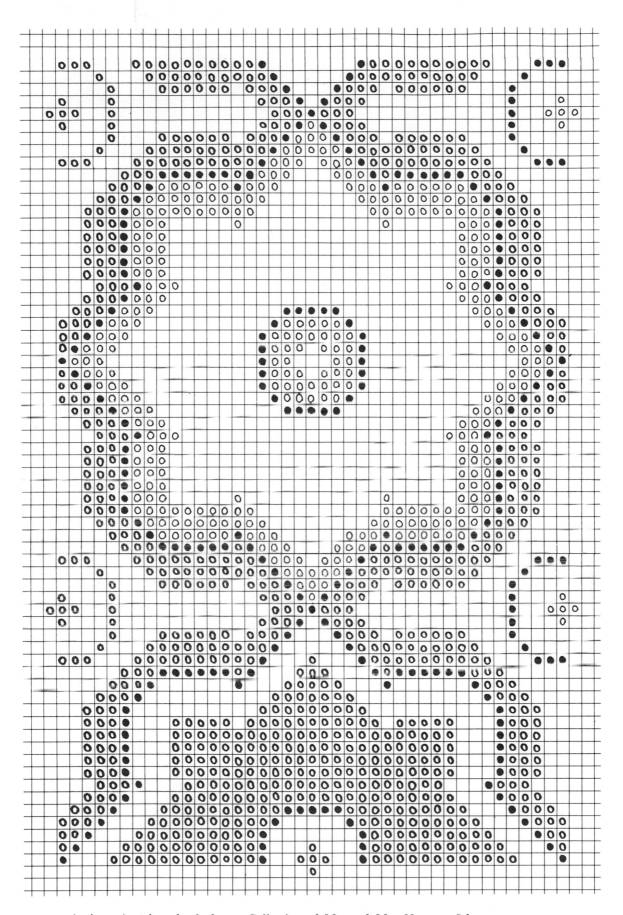

JESSICA. Antique American hooked rug. Collection of Mr. and Mrs. Norman Schneyer.

56

JOSHUA. Antique American hooked rug. Collection of Mr. and Mrs. Sol Zaret. (See color plate 8)

BETTY. Hooked rug designed and made by Monica Carl.

THE HOBBIT. Hooked rug designed and made by Shulamith Miller.

ABSTRACT. Hooked stair runner designed and made by Mimi Waldhorn.

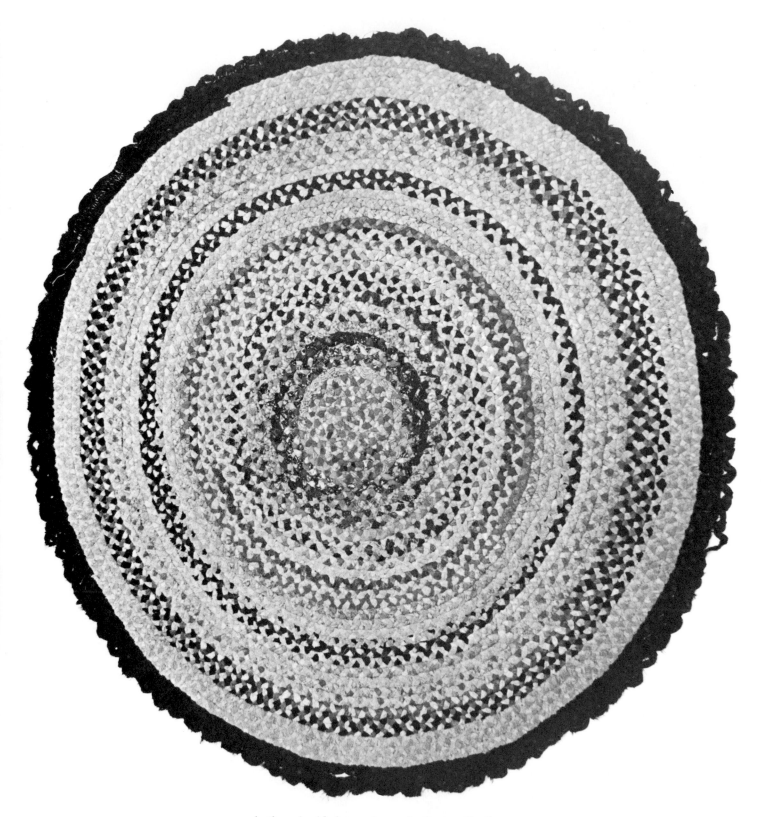

Antique braided round rug. Author's collection.

3 BRAIDED RUGS

HISTORY

The skill of braiding came naturally to women who, from the time they were young girls, braided their hair without even looking at what they were doing. Braiding was even popular with young boys who playfully twisted straw or hemp into braids. The first braided rugs were probably made of straw and were used to keep feet off damp earth floors. Later, when fabric was woven and used for clothing, worn scraps of well-used coats, suits, and dresses were saved and cut and wound into balls to be used for the rugs. Braided rugs were very popular with the colonists. Today they are still popular, although a great many of the braided rugs that we see now are machine-made of new or reprocessed fabrics. Their popularity is due to the fact that they are long-wearing, colorful, are thick enough to stay in place on the floor, lie flat, and feel soft underfoot.

The Shape of Your Rug

Select a shape that best suits your purpose. The oldest braided rugs I have seen are round. As people became adept at this most simple form, they started to experiment with other shapes, such as oval and square rugs.

EQUIPMENT

Braiding requires few tools to create a truly beautiful and useful rug. You need only big safety pins, scissors, thimble, needle, heavy thread (preferably linen or shoemaker floss), sewing thread, lacer, long-nosed pliers, yardstick, tailor's chalk, and fabric.

Fabric

Heavy or medium-weight woolens are best for durable large rugs. A lightweight wool is suitable for small rugs. I don't recommend cottons, as they do not wear well, but if you want to make a small kitchen or bath mat, washable cotton could serve that purpose.

If you prefer using new fabric (which will end up being rather expensive), try to contact a manufacturer who will sell you remnants by the pound. If you are satisfied with used fabrics, many sources are available. Aside from your own old coats, suits, skirts, and blankets, you might press your friends and relatives into service. Tell them you are looking for a particular color wool. Somehow a specific request gets better results than a general one. Once I was making a rug with all shades of brown. When word got around, my friends swamped me with all their old woolens in every shade of beige to brown imaginable. People like to try to identify their old clothes in the finished rug.

Rummage sales are also a good source for woolens. A few years ago I was able to buy a heavy wool skirt for five cents. Prices have gone up, but they are still not prohibitive.

Remove all signs of worn fabric before you start to cut your fabric. All moth holes should be cut out so that they will not weaken your rug. If you hold the fabric up to a sunny window and examine it closely, you will see where the wear spots and moth holes are.

Try to find closely woven fabrics, as they will wear better. Knitted fabrics have too much give and should be avoided.

Before you attempt to use old clothing, remove any zippers, buttons, linings, collars, cuffs, and pockets. Open darts, cut along seams, and then throw clothing into a washing machine or wash by hand in cool water with a mild detergent or soap. This will soften the fabric as well as clean it. Dry and avoid pressing. Do not dry wool in a dryer; it will mat. Drying on an outdoor line is most desirable. Apartment dwellers should drip-dry wool overnight on a rack in the bathtub.

PREPARATION

Cutting Strips

The fabric must first be cut into strips. The thickness of your finished rug will depend on the weight and width of these strips. If your fabric is medium or heavy, 2½ inches is a good width.

For lightweight rugs (which don't wear as well) lightweight fabrics can be used in 2-inch strips. Use only lightweight materials in a lightweight rug, and medium to heavyweight in a heavyweight rug. Do not mix the two if you want your heavyweight rug to last.

Tearing strips is usually fast and accurate if your fabric allows it with a minimum of raveling. Be sure to tear with the grain of the fabric. If you cut strips, use a yardstick and tailor's chalk to mark your fabric the proper width. Always cut with the grain of the fabric so that you end up with the longest possible strip from each piece of fabric. There are commercial cutters on the market which will cut your material up to 2 inches wide. Some come with a combination blade that may be used for cutting narrower strips for hooking rugs.

Sewing Strips

In order to braid with a minimum of trouble, strips should be approximately 10 feet long. This is accomplished by sewing together strips of matching colors. Place one end over another and sew diagonally across strips so that a bias is made. Cut each seam ¼ inch from the stitching line. You may sew these strips by hand; however, sewing them by machine will add strength to the rug.

Once you have sewn together 10 feet of fabric, you should roll the length into a ball. This will allow for efficient storage and easy handling when you are ready to use it.

Folding Strips

Folding is a very important step in the making of a braided rug. If your strips are not folded neatly with all raw edges hidden, your finished rug will not be very neat looking.

Fold outside edges (lengthwise) so that they meet in the center. The right side of the fabric should now be the only side visible. Now fold again so that the first folded edges meet. You will have four thicknesses throughout the strip.

In order to maintain these folds there are several methods that can be used:

You can pin the folds and then baste them very loosely so that the stitches won't pull when you work on the braiding.

You can use a steam iron to press folds on lightweight material, but be careful and press very lightly or else the strips will be too flat.

You can buy a gadget called a braid-aid in any needlework shop which will automatically fold fabric as you braid. You will need three of these—one for each braid. These are best used on narrow strips of lightweight material and are slipped down along strips as you work.

You can fold as you braid. You will get used to this method as you continue to braid. However, until you are experienced, prefolding is easier.

Whatever method you choose, you must then roll the strips into coils or wheels. Before starting the actual braiding, prepare as many

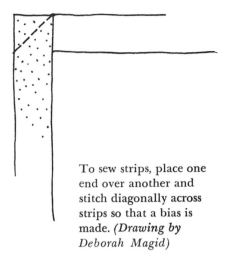

To sew strips, place one end over another and stitch diagonally across strips so that a bias is made. *(Drawing by Deborah Magid)*

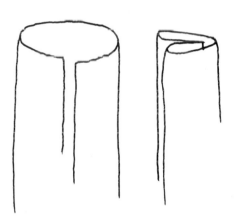

Folded strips *(Drawings by Deborah Magid)*

63

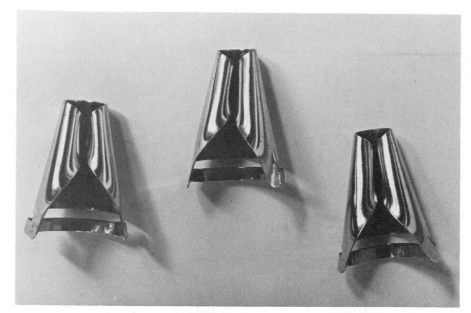

Coiled folded strips

coils as you possibly can. In order to maintain folds, dampen each coil slightly by filling a shallow soup dish with no more than ⅛ inch of water and dipping the coil into it, first one side, then another. Blot on a clean towel and allow to dry thoroughly. It is not absolutely necessary to have all your fabric prepared before you begin, but the more you have, the easier your color planning will be.

Color

Try to separate your materials into three groups:
1. Light or neutral colors—tan, beige, light gray, etc.
2. Bright colors
3. Dark colors—navy, black, dark brown, dark grays

The traditional three-strand braid for rugs consists of two dull or dark colors and one bright one. The two dull or dark colors could include one tweed or plaid and one solid; or two solid colors; or one tweed and one checked; or one tweed and one plaid. The light or bright color could be any color you want to use that fits into your color scheme or, if you are using old fabrics, whatever you have available.

Shaded rugs were popular in the New Hampshire mountains. These rugs have light centers and progress to dark borders. Usually only one or two colors in their various tones and shades were used. To make a rug that is neither light nor dark, use one strand of light, one medium, and one dark throughout and gradually darken as you get near the outer edge. Just be sure you have enough of each color to make a complete round, remembering that the further you progress, the larger the round will be. You will lose about 1 foot every 4 feet you braid. For example: You will need 15 feet of strips to make a 12-foot braid.

PROCEDURES

Starting to Braid

For a three-strand braid, release about 4 feet from each of your three folded rolls of fabric. Use large safety pins to keep strips from unrolling further. Using the same bias seam you used to make your length of strips, sew two strands together. Place joined strips in a straight line, lying flat with seam facing you. Now place the end of the third folded strip (with the seam facing left) onto the first two strips between fold as shown in illustration. Sew sturdily.

To hold the ends in place while you are braiding, tack joined strips to a tabletop or board or anchor between your knees. There are commercial clamps made for this purpose which screw onto a table and are similar to a vise. You are now ready to start braiding. As your first braid will be the center of your rug, be extra careful to work neatly. Be sure that your open edges are kept to the left as you work. (This is so very important. I must keep repeating it.)

Remember that braiding differs from plaiting. Braid—*do not* plait —in order to be able to lace together all open ends so that they will never show. Keep thumb and nails showing. If you turn your wrist and your thumbnails go down, your open edge will not remain facing left at all times.

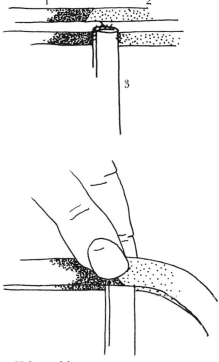

Using a bias seam, sew two strands (1 and 2) together. Place and stitch the third strand (3) as shown. Fold 1 and 2 over 3.

To Braid

Lift the right strand over the center strand and lay it down, keeping your thumbnail showing. Then lift the left strand over the new center strand and lay it down with thumbnail showing, then the right over the center, etc., always being careful to keep the tension the same for each stroke you make. Keep your thumbnails up! Note that each time you change the position of a strand, you are creating a new left, a new right, etc. If you follow these directions carefully (keeping seams always to the left) you will have no trouble with this straight braiding, and after you begin your rug with the first few modified square turns, the rest of the rug is done with the straight braiding. Try not to have strips end at the same point, so that when you attach a new strand the seams will not be lumped together. When you do attach the new strips, do it with a bias seam, making certain that the seams are facing left.

Braiding

Braiding:
(a) Overlap three times.
(b) Place center strand over left strand.
(c) Fold right strand up over center and fold center strand down.

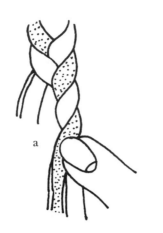 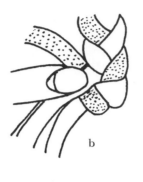 

a b c

Modified Square Turns

Where you place your modified square turns will, of course, depend on the shape of the rug you are making, as it is these turns that keep the rug perfectly flat. In a round rug you will need about 12 of these modified square turns. In an oval rug you will need 3 at each end, and in a square rug, one modified square turn is done at each corner. Exact placement of the turns is explained more specifically in the instructions for making oval, round, and square rugs (see below).

These turns will increase the loops on one side of the braid so that the strands maintain an evenly braided appearance when they are laced together to make the actual rug. For a modified square turn, instead of straight braiding, lift the right strand over the center strand, the new right over the new center again, and the new right over the new center again a final third time. Now tightly place the center strand under the left strand. Next fold the right hand strand up over the center strand, then fold the center strand down and continue the regular braid.

Making an Oval Rug

Decide on the width and length of the rug you are prepared to make. Subtract the width from the length. This will be the length of the center piece. For example, for a finished rug size 3 by 5 feet, the center piece will be 2 feet long. For a 9- by 12-foot rug, the center piece will be 3 feet long.

Make a *T* start and begin with regular braiding. When you reach the length you need for the center piece, do 3 modified square turns in succession, then straight braid back to the beginning *T* start and do 3 more modified square turns. The rest of the rug is straight braiding.

Making a Round Rug

Make a *T* start, then do 12 modified square turns. The rest of the rug again is straight braiding.

Center detail of braided oval rug

Starting a square rug
(*Drawing by Deborah Magid*)

Making a Square Rug

Make a *T* start, make two square corners, one right after the other, straight braiding once, then modified turn, straight braiding down the length, modified turn, straight braiding, etc. When braiding a square rug, you must begin lacing almost up to each turn so that you know exactly when to make the turn. Remember when you lace to *skip* that loop that you pulled tightly. This will keep your corner sharp and your loops will fall into the correct position on each side.

Color Changes

Changing colors every few rows in about the same place each time will give a patterned effect. On an oval rug change colors on the curves. Colonial rugs, however, were multicolored, for the women added any color they were able to spare. For this effect, colors are added at any time to any strand.

Lacing

Lacing braids together rather than sewing them is an easy method for assembling your rug. It is also stronger than sewing and won't necessitate constant repairs. Some of my very old braided rugs, which were sewn together, rip apart every time I lift them.

Another method used by women many years ago was to work the third strand of their braid right through the previous round, using a rug or crochet hook. In this way they eliminated the additional step of sewing. It is not easy and I don't recommend it unless you are a talented adventurer.

For a lacing I like to use shoemaker floss or linen thread (avoid any waxed threads, as these tend to cut into your braids) and a flat, broad lacer, which is a large flat needle with a curved point.

As you lace, interlock your braids—rather than having loops side by side, have loop between loop. No threads will show, the rug will look woven, and you can pull the loops together very closely. An added asset is that you will have a reversible rug!

Start with open folds facing left toward the center of the rug. Knot the cord and tuck the knot between the folds. Insert the lacing needle into a space on the rug with an upward stroke, pick up a loop on the braid with a down stroke. The next up stroke should pick up the adjacent strand of the adjacent braid. This will interlock your braids.

Lacer

Skip one loop at a time on the curves of an oval or round rug but *never* skip on straight sides. This is called increasing and is always done on the braid you are attaching. If you increase (or skip) too much, the rug will ripple. Three increases on each side of a curve or six for the whole curve is average. Mark each increase with a pin so that you don't have them in the same spot on each curve. As the rug gets larger, there will be more loops between the skips. If the curves of the braid seem too full and start to pucker, avoid increasing for one round.

Use thread 2 to 3 feet in length, and when you run out of thread, simply connect the new piece to the old one, using a square knot, see illustration 7, cut two ends and keep going.

Square knot
(*Drawing by Deborah Magid*)

FINISHING

Tapering

Tapering is used to end off the rug made with a continuous braid. About 6 inches from where you want the braid to end, put aside the strips, leaving an 18-inch length. Reduce the width of these strips to about one half. Unfold the strips and start cutting at the end of the strip from the center of the width and gradually come out to the full width at the point where you stopped braiding. Refold the strips.

Braid the tapered strips to within 6 inches of the end, ending with a right-hand stroke. Your braid should be about half the normal width. Continue lacing this tapered braid to the last loop on the braid. Make sure that the last loop ends on the *indent* of the braid of the former row. Lace in reverse for about 6 inches to fasten the lacing thread. With long-nosed pliers pull the first end into the space that the last loop of braid was laced into and weave it into the rug for a few inches. Cut off the excess strip concealing the end.

Now on the other side of the rug, pull the next strand into the rug and out on the other side. Weave this end into this side. Cut off excess and conceal the end under a loop. On the other side, again pull the last strip into the next space on the rug and weave and cut as for the others.

When weaving, do not pull all three strips into the same space or you will have a bump. On an oval rug end on a curve rather than a straight edge.

Try to keep all your braids the same width or you will find that your rug will ripple. Work on a table or the floor so that you can keep the rug flat as you work.

There are many combinations and variations you may use with your braids. The following drawings will give you some ideas:

Rectangle using continuous braid with modified squares corners.

Rectangle done in strips. Unbraid 3 inches at each end to form a fringe. Stitch down on underside along ends of braid to avoid raveling of braiding. If you don't want fringe, sew braids all around the rectangle.

A traditional three-and-three rug is made with 3 strips of braid of one color family sewn together, then 1 strip of a dark color, then 3 strips of another color family, then dark braid again.

Some women hooked the whole center of a rug and then used borders of braiding.

Rectangle formed from four or five ovals. Make four or five small oval rugs. Attach on sides of length.

A *panel rug* consists of braided rugs 18 to 20 inches wide which are sewn together, with a few rows of braids around the edge.

A *wheel rug* is not simple, but if you are ambitious, you will have an unusual rug. Start with an oval rug about 12 x 27 inches. Then make enough 12-inch braided circles to surround the center. Next, sew the

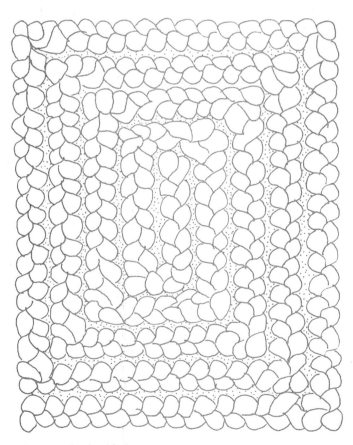

Rectangular braided rug
(*Drawing by Deborah Magid*)

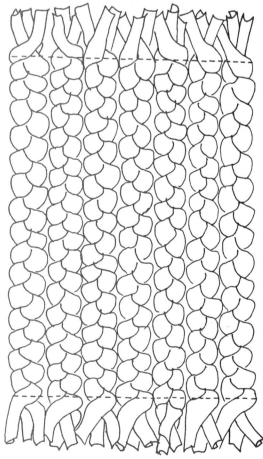

Rectangle done in strips
(*Drawing by Deborah Magid*)

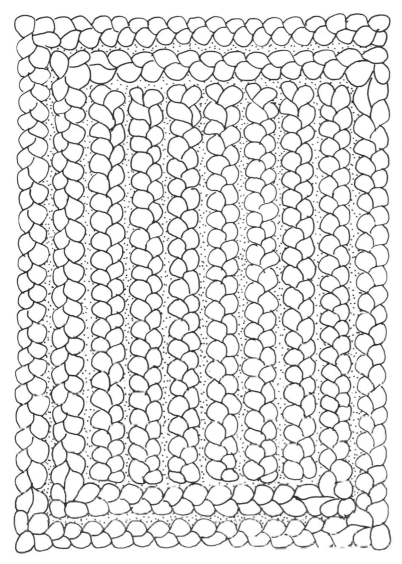

Rectangle done in strips with braid around edges *(Drawing by Deborah Magid)*

Three-and-three rug *(Drawing by Deborah Magid)*

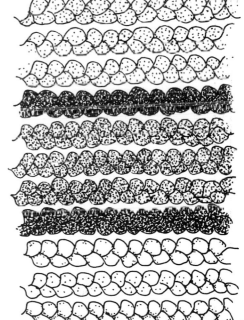

circles to the center and attach sides of each circle to one another. Next, sew borders of braid, preferably of a dark color, around the edges of the small circles. Use as many rows as you need.

Three small, round rugs are sewn together, then 6 or 7 braids go all around them to form an unusual braided rug.

A *cloverleaf rug,* popular in early New England days, was a clever combination of braiding and hooking. It consists of 3 small, round braided rugs attached to each other in the form of a cloverleaf. To fill in the opening in the center, sew a piece of canvas backing on the underside and hook a deep pile center. Finish by sewing 2 or 3 braids around the entire edge of the rug.

In rural Pennsylvania a combination of hooking and braiding was also popular. Braided rounds were arranged on a loosely woven textile base and hooked in between them.

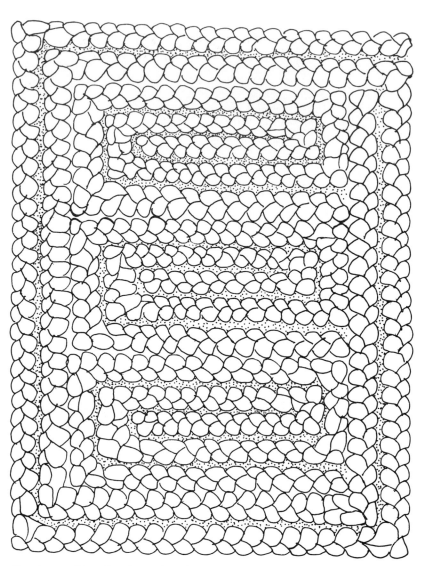

Panel rug *(Drawing by Deborah Magid)*

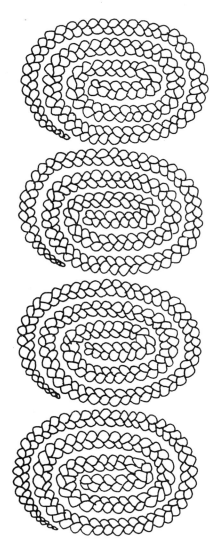

Four ovals connected to make a rectangle *(Drawing by Deborah Magid)*

Wheel rug *(Drawing by Deborah Magid)*

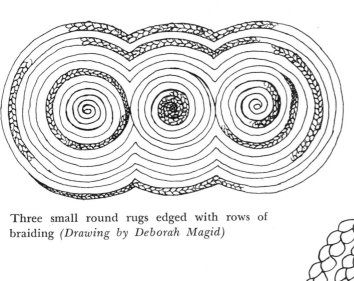

Three small round rugs edged with rows of braiding *(Drawing by Deborah Magid)*

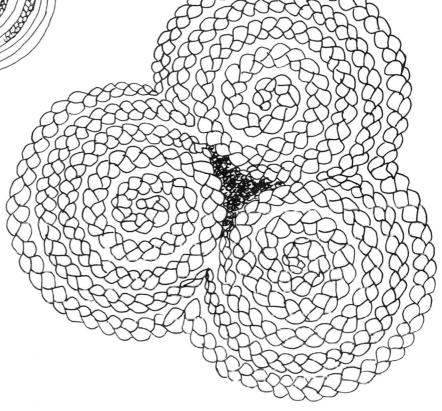

Clover leaf with hooking *(Drawing by Deborah Magid)*

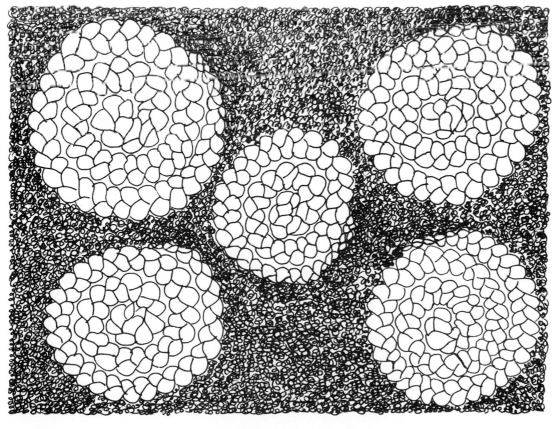

Hooking and braiding combined *(Drawing by Deborah Magid)*

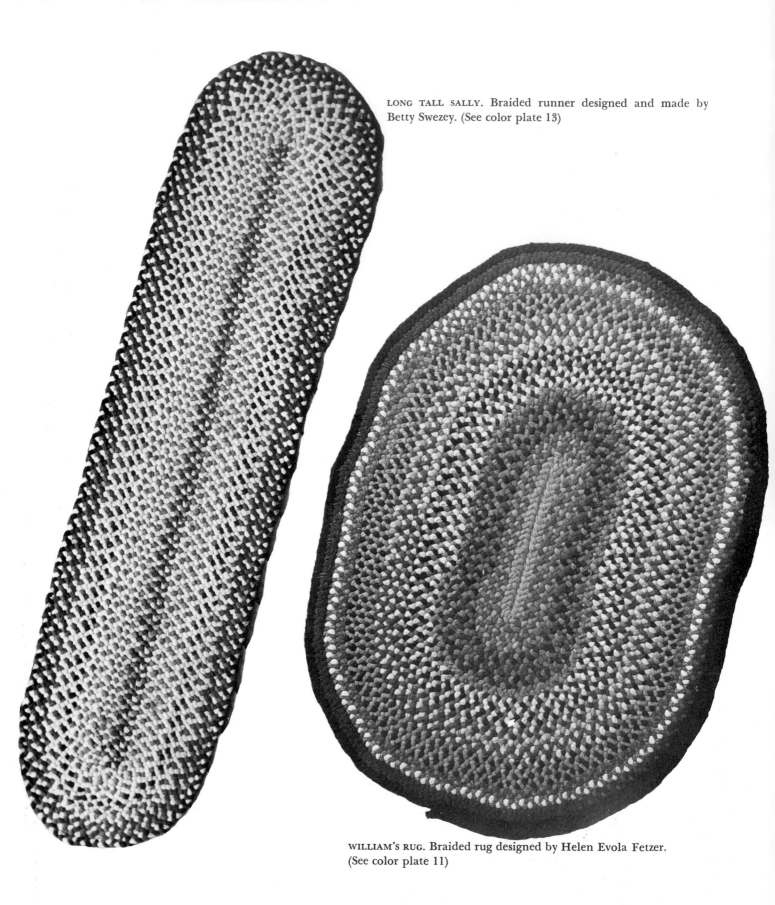

LONG TALL SALLY. Braided runner designed and made by Betty Swezey. (See color plate 13)

WILLIAM'S RUG. Braided rug designed by Helen Evola Fetzer. (See color plate 11)

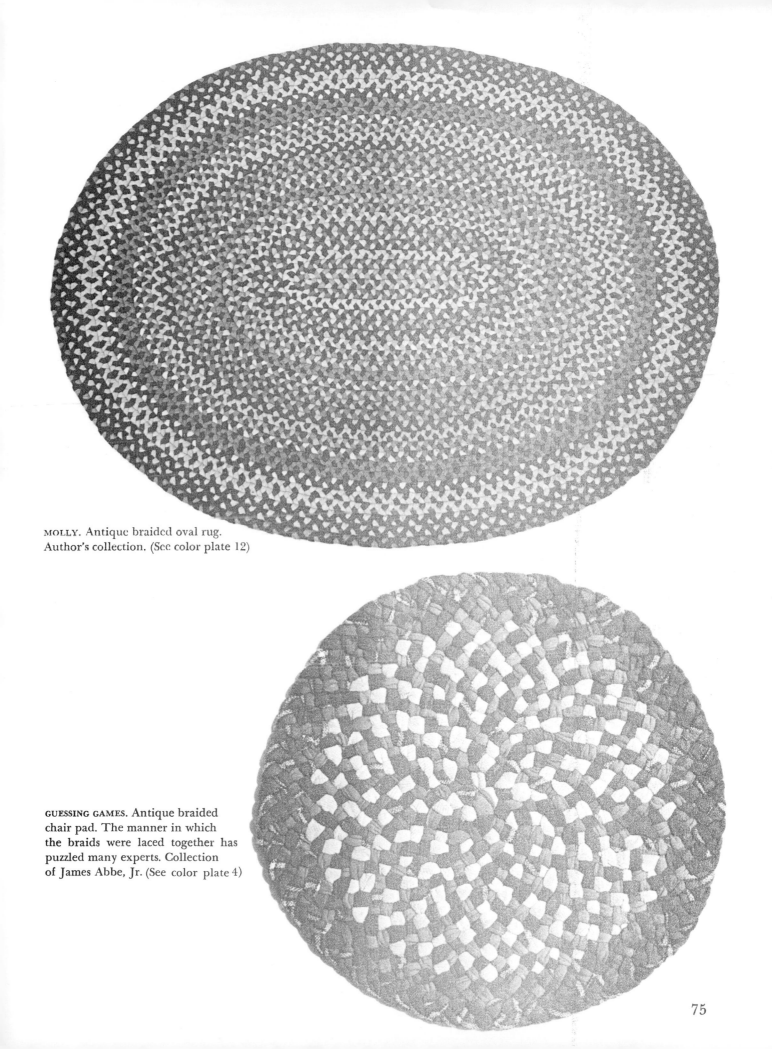

MOLLY. Antique braided oval rug.
Author's collection. (See color plate 12)

GUESSING GAMES. Antique braided
chair pad. The manner in which
the braids were laced together has
puzzled many experts. Collection
of James Abbe, Jr. (See color plate 4)

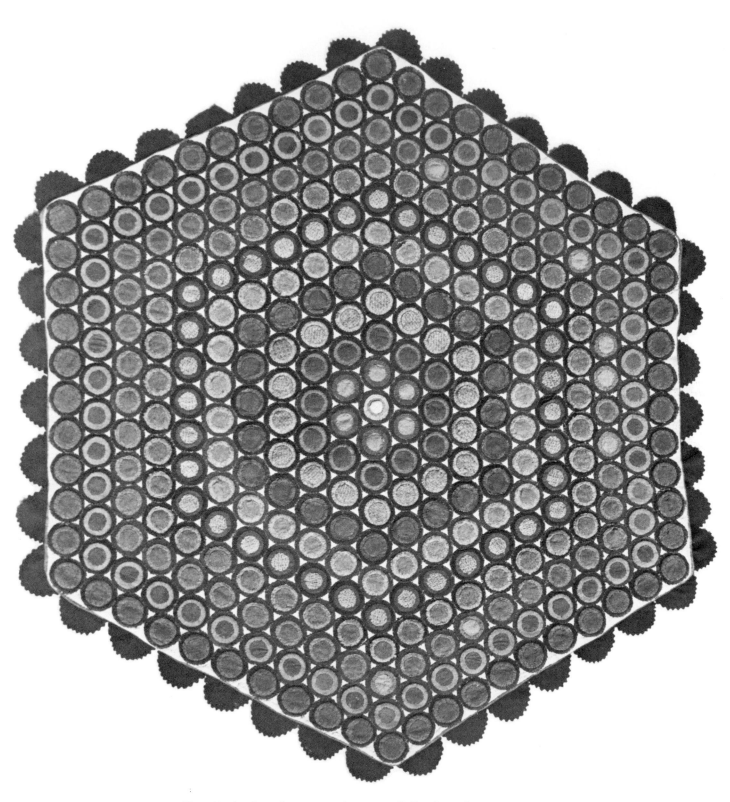

HEXAGON. New England antique pen wiper rug. Collection of James Abbe, Jr. New England, circa 1880. (See color plate 15)

4 PEN WIPER RUG

The antique rug shown here is a hexagon to which three varying-sized circles are attached, forming a simple pattern. It is called a pen wiper rug because in the old days, before ballpoints and even fountain pens were used, pens dipped in inkwells had to be wiped frequently. The traditional pen wipers were composed of three layers of cloth (wool, felt, or cotton) just like the little circles on this rug.

Pen wiper or "cotton" rugs are made with strong backings. Monk's cloth is a good choice. Felt is also used, as it requires no edging. Cut backing to the size and shape you require. Hem if necessary. Make three different-sized circular patterns. Perhaps a half dollar, a quarter, and a nickel will do. You will be placing the three different circles on top of each other: largest on bottom, medium-sized in the center, and smallest on top. On this rug the dark color is at the bottom and the other two circles vary.

There are two ways to sew the circles together. You can fasten the three with a French knot through the center and buttonhole only the largest to the backing, or you can use the blanket or buttonhole stitch to attach each circle to the next in size. Whichever you decide to use, first lay out your colors on the backing to plan your general design and color scheme. This rug has an edging of pinked semicircles sewn onto the underside of the backing. (See color plate 15)

WENDY. Designed and made by Dubby Wassyng.

5 RYA RUGS

History

The literal translation of Swedish *rya,* Finnish *rijijy,* or Norse *Ryer* is "rugs," although rug does not accurately describe the multiple functions of this popular item. Janice Stewart in her book, *Folk Arts of Norway,* says that the

> . . . earliest ryer looked like animal pelts and were doubtless a substitution for these. On the west coast where ryer went to sea with fisherman and hence needed to be able to withstand the salt water, they held up much better than animal skins, which soon rotted under the constant wetting from sea spray. Women folk of the coastal regions took the long smooth and wiry hairs from their local breed of sheep and spun them very loosely into thread which, when used undyed, formed a pile that looked like fur.

In those days the yarns weren't washed, and the natural oils in the wool shed water easily, so the fishermen used the ryas as raincoats. They were also hung on the wall to keep out draughts. Later they were used as floor coverings, sleigh robes, and pillow covers.

Rya are knotted pile rugs similar to shag rugs. The rya knot is derived from the Oriental or Ghiordes knot. The pile varies from $\frac{1}{2}$ to $4\frac{1}{2}$ inches. If the pile is very short, the effect is less shaggy and more Oriental in character.

Originally rya rugs were made on looms. Each knot was tied in a row separated by several threads of weft. See the chapter on weaving for a more detailed description of this procedure.

Today the most popular type of rya is needlemade on ready woven backings from Scandinavia which are readily available here.

Rya backing from Scandinavia

Equipment

Backing Foundation

Rya backing from Scandinavia has the weft (horizontal threads) already woven in place with the open warp (vertical) threads showing about every half inch. This foundation comes in widths from 17 up to 47 inches. Some even come in precut rug sizes with finished edges and fringe already on. If you buy backing by the yard, try to buy the exact width so that you won't have to finish the selvages. When figuring size, allow about 3 inches all around the design for finishing, unless you make use of the selvages.

Needlepoint canvas can be used if you separate the rows of rya knots with rows of long-legged cross-stitch. These stitches will be invisible in the finished rug. Use 3 rows of long-legged cross-stitch for a 2-inch pile and 4 rows for a 2½-inch pile. Work 3 rows of long-legged cross-stitches along both selvages to prevent pile from falling beyond edges. You can prepare the needlepoint canvas with the long-legged cross-stitch before you start to knot. See chapter on embroidered rugs for directions for long-legged cross-stitch (p. 111).

Needles

Heavy rug needles 2¾ inches long with blunted tips will hold the multiple strands required for the rya. Try to have enough needles for each color so they can be threaded and ready for use when you need them.

Yarn

Two-ply rya yarns from Scandinavia are available in most needlework shops. They are all wool and have a tightly twisted ropelike look. The colors are spectacular and offer a wide range from which to choose. The yarns come in skeins and are sold by weight. There are two weights: a heavier one for rugs and a lighter weight for wall hangings or pillows. It is interesting to combine different weights of yarn in one rug. After you have learned the technique, try a combination of yarns, even varying the pile heights within the design.

Cut through the skein of yarn on only one side so that you will have long lengths with which to work, or unwind the skein into a ball and cut from this. The number of strands you decide to use for knotting will depend on the weight of the yarn, the tightness of the backing, and the closeness of the knots. Four strands will usually make a rather full rya.

Yarn Quantity

It is difficult to make a general statement about quantity. It will vary according to the type of backing, the weight of the wool, the height of the pile, and the closeness of the knots. A general rule is $\frac{1}{2}$ pound for every square foot of 2-inch pile.

Whatever the quantity you figure you will need, buy some extra. It is frustrating to run out of yarn. If you should run short of a color and can't find the same dye lot, mix the new color with strands of the old color for a few rows and even *you* won't know the difference when the rug is finished.

Rya rugs are expensive to make, as the long pile uses much more yarn than a short pile or flat-stitch rug, and you should use top quality yarn. Once you invest time and effort, don't use materials that will not stand up under use.

Pile Gauge

If you want all the knots to be of even lengths, use a pile gauge. The yarn is wrapped around the gauge for each stitch, then cut along a slot in the gauge with a razor blade. Gauges are available in rug-supply stores or you can make one yourself.

I have often used three fingers as a gauge to control the pile height. You can even use your thumb if you want a short pile.

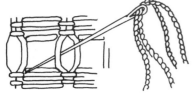

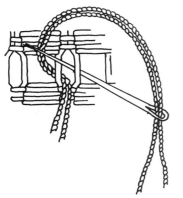

Insert the needle from front to back between vertical warp threads.

Bring the needle up through the backing to the left of the warp threads. Insert needle to the right of the warp threads from back to front. Bring the needle out between threads from back to front. Pull to form a knot.

(Drawings by Deborah Magid)

PROCEDURES

If you have decided to use 4 strands of yarn, thread 2 long strands through the needle, then fold them in half. This will give you a 4-strand knot. If you are using Scandinavian rug backing, leave the first row of backing empty. The pile will cover it. Start the next row at the left and continue working across from left to right until you reach the end of your design. (Work from right to left if you are left-handed.)

Each knot will be tied around a group of 2 to 4 threads of the backing, depending upon how thick you want the rug to be.

THE RYA OR GHIORDES KNOT

Insert your needle from the front to the back between warp threads. Hold onto the tail of the first knot at the length your pile will be. Bring the needle up through the backing to the left of the warp threads. Insert the needle to the right of the two threads from the front to the back and bring the needle out between them from back to front. Now pull tight to form a knot. Remember that the needle always moves from right to left. If you are using a gauge to measure the pile, wrap the yarn around the gauge before starting your next knot.

Continue across the rug in this way until you come to a color change. Cut yarn after the last knot so that the pile is the proper height. Cut through all the loops that are on the gauge. It is easier to cut loops as you go along rather than leave the whole job for the end when the chances of missing some loops are greater. Start the new color the same way you started before. Remember to leave a tail of the proper length on the first knot.

Wrap the yarn around the gauge before you start each knot.

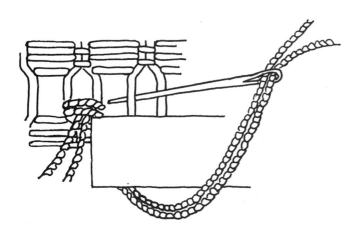

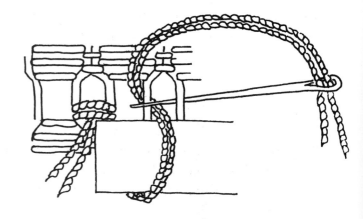

DESIGNS

Many of the rya designs that follow can be used for latch hooked, hooked, or embroidered rugs. Additional rya rugs are pictured in color plates 16 and 17.

ARCADIA

To copy this rug, start by tracing a circle in the center of your backing fabric. Draw freehand lines around it above and below as shown in the photograph. The edges have almost straight lines. Use shades of one color ranging from almost white to black, brown, or navy. This design can be done as a latch hook rug also.

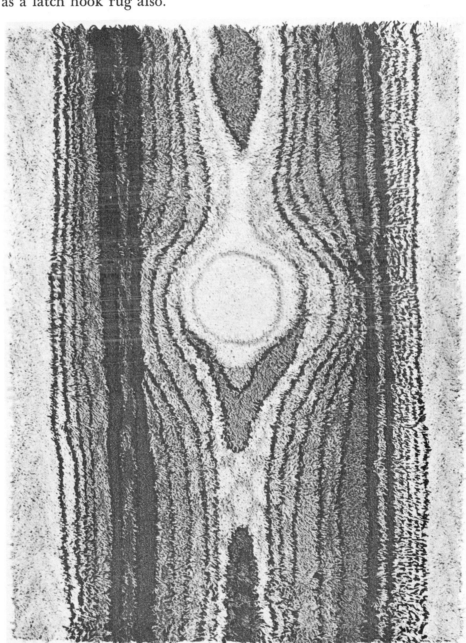

ARCADIA. Designed and manufactured by Egetaepper, Inc., Denmark.

84

PAPYRUS. Designed and manufactured by Egetaepper, Inc., Denmark. This rug can be made any size that you require. This pattern is also suitable for latch hooked rugs.

86

CYPRESS. Repeat pattern as often as necessary. This pattern can be used for latch hooking also.
Designed and manufactured by Egetaepper, Inc., Denmark.

MOONSONG. This modern design is made with bright colors and outlined in black. It can be used for latch hooked, hooked, and embroidered rugs as well.

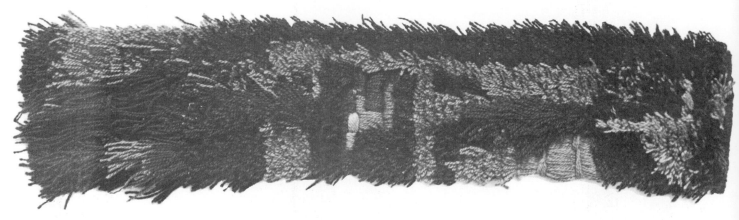

AND SO IT GOES. Rya wall hanging designed by Ellen and Kenneth Katz and made by Kenneth Katz. Note how the long pile is held down by cross-threads.

NORWAY. Designed and made by Dubby Wassyng. The subtle use of color blends makes this simple design an interesting rug.

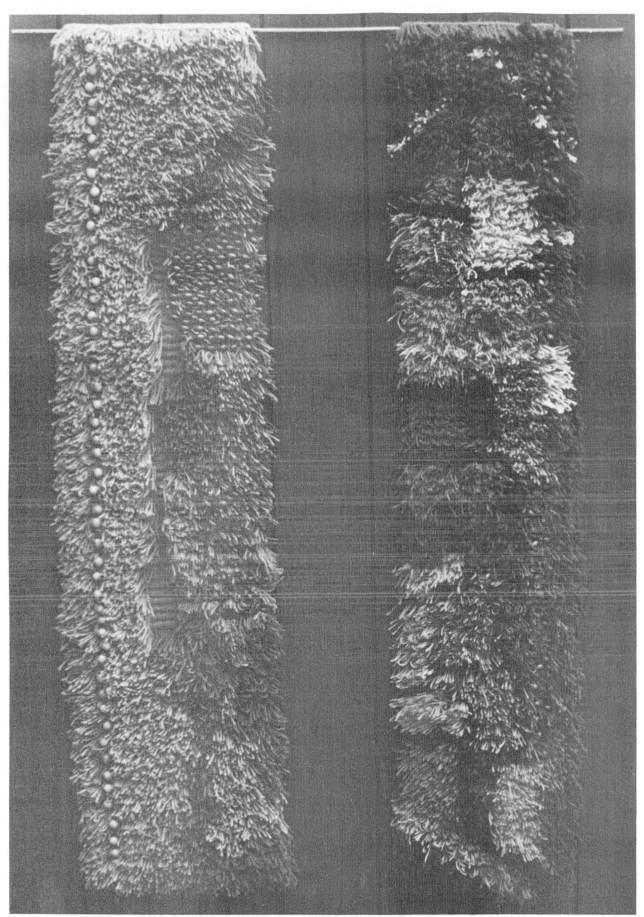

TOLAR (left). Rya wall hanging made of flat seam and beads. PATCHWORK (right). Rya wall hanging made of cut and uncut yarn. Both designed and made by Daga Ramsey.

SHEEP. Latch hooked rug designed and made by Minna Zaret. Instructions on page 97. (See color plate 20)

6 LATCH HOOKED RUGS

HISTORY

Latch or latchet hooking has recently become a popular form of rug making. Actually, latched rugs are knotted rather than looped like traditional hooked rugs. With the aid of a latch hook, knots are made on a backing canvas with precut pieces of yarn. The results are dense, lush, cut pile rugs with nice resiliency underfoot.

The latch rug is easily portable, since it is not necessary to work on a frame.

The finished latch rug looks much like a rya except that the pile is knotted along every row.

Designs are usually large and lack tiny details. The height of the pile can vary within a rug, making sculptural effects possible.

Because making the knot itself is foolproof with the latch, it has become a popular family project. Anyone can pick it up and work a few rows and still have a uniform-looking pile.

EQUIPMENT

Backing Canvas

The canvas used for latch rugs must be an open-mesh, cross-hatched fabric that forms squares. The best is a penelope rug canvas, which is double-threaded—two wefts and two warps. The warp threads run parallel to the selvages and are twisted around the weft threads. This double thread makes a durable foundation for the rug.

Penelope rug canvas comes in various widths ranging from 12 to 48 inches. Try to get the width you need so that you can use the selvages without cutting them, thus eliminating two raw edges. The

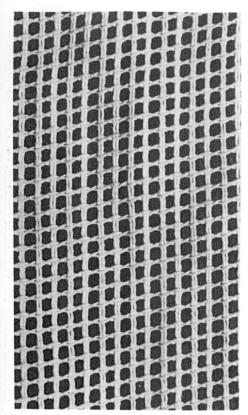
Latch hook backing canvas

number of spaces per inch varies also. I usually use a 4- or 5-to-the-inch canvas, which produces a thick pile. Of course, the type of yarn you use also is a factor in the density of the finished rug.

To prepare your canvas, cut a piece that will allow for at least a 1½-inch border on all sides. To prevent raveling, fold masking tape along the raw edges.

If you want to make a rug that is larger than the available canvas, you can join two pieces of canvas before or after you hook. To join before hooking, align the two sections so that the selvages run in the same direction. Cut off the selvages of the ends to be joined. Lap one piece over the other for about 2 inches, being very careful to match the threads and spaces. With heavy thread, whip stitch the top to the bottom on each end. When you hook, you will go through the double layer, making it impossible for the canvas to separate.

If you don't want to carry a large canvas or find it bulky to handle, you can leave a 2-inch piece unhooked at the end and beginning of the pieces to be joined. When you have hooked both sections, proceed as above, hooking through both layers of canvas. Caution: Latch hooking is all done in one direction, so don't start at opposite ends of separate sections. See instructions that follow. Also, you will not be losing 2 inches of your pattern from *each* section, only 1 inch on each end.

Yarn

Almost any rug yarn that fits through the mesh can be used for latch hooking. I always use wool. It wears well, is resilient, and looks best. You can mix types of yarn for an interesting effect.

The easiest yarn to use comes in precut lengths, about 2½ inches long, loosely twisted in 4, 5, or 6 plies. These packs are put out by different manufacturers and usually have about 350 pieces in a pack. Unfortunately, these precut packs are much more expensive than uncut yarn and sometimes do not come in a complete color range.

I buy rug yarn by the pound. I have used rya-type yarns, weaving yarns, and sometimes even knitting yarns. With knitting yarns use multiple strands for each knot to compensate for the lighter weight. Also, if you are using it because you need a particular color that is not available in any other yarn, use it only in small areas. It will not hold up as well as rug yarn. Remember that you can always dye the yarn.

With the precut 350-piece packs of yarn, you should be able to latch hook about 20 square inches. It is easy to calculate the amount of yarn you will need by counting the number of knots in a square inch of your canvas. When you cut your own, the amount of yarn that you need will depend upon the length of your pile and the weight of your wool. If your pile is 1 inch high, one ounce will cover about 20 square inches. Estimate the number of square inches for each color, then buy some extra. I never feel unhappy about leftover yarn, since it inspires me to make other rugs using leftovers.

Cutting the yarn to size is easy and sometimes is a pleasant change from the latching. Wind the skein into a ball. Make a gauge from wood or stiff, folded cardboard that will give you the desired length. Remember that you will use ½ inch for the knot alone and the pile is doubled. So, if your strand is cut 2½ inches long, your pile will be 1 inch high. Experiment with the pile height before you make your gauge. Cut a few pieces of different lengths and make a latched knot. When you are satisfied with one, take it out and measure the length. Then make your gauge. I use a piece of wood about 1 foot long on which I make a groove to allow the scissors to glide along freely. Wind the yarn around the gauge in a single layer and cut along the groove. Continue winding and cutting until you have enough of each color to start hooking. You may decide to use different pile heights throughout sections of the rug for effect.

Latch Hook

There are slight differences in latch hooks depending upon their manufacturers, but basically, they have plastic or wooden handles, long shanks, either straight or curved, hooks at the end, and free-swinging latches that help make the knot. When you buy one, try out straight and curved shanks to see which you are more comfortable using.

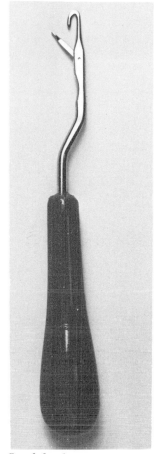

Latch hook

PROCEDURES

Latch hooking is a simple technique. Once you master it, you will develop a rhythm that will increase your speed and make latch hooking a delight.

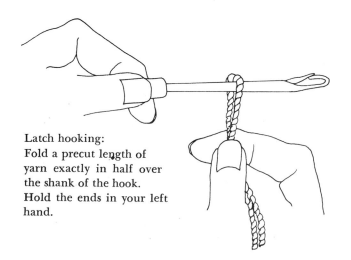

Latch hooking: Fold a precut length of yarn exactly in half over the shank of the hook. Hold the ends in your left hand.

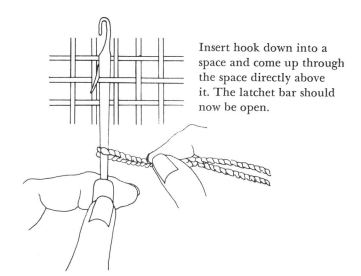

Insert hook down into a space and come up through the space directly above it. The latchet bar should now be open.

95

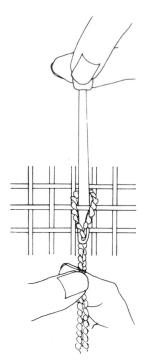

Put both loose ends of
yarn under the hook.

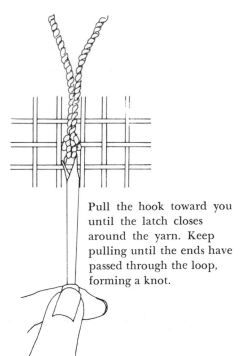

Pull the hook toward you
until the latch closes
around the yarn. Keep
pulling until the ends have
passed through the loop,
forming a knot.

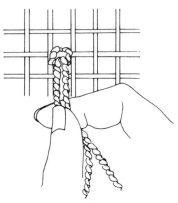

Tighten the knot by
pulling the ends by hand.

Practice a few knots on sample fabric before you start on your rug.

Fold a precut length of yarn exactly in half over the shank of the hook. Hold the ends in your left hand.

Insert the hook down into a space and come up through the space directly above it. The latchet bar should now be open.

Put both loose ends of yarn under the hook, and while holding these ends, pull the hook toward you until the latch closes around the yarn. Now let go of the ends and keep pulling until the ends have passed through the loop, forming a knot.

Tighten the knot by pulling the ends by hand.

When you start your rug, start in the lower left-hand corner. If you are left-handed, start in the lower right-hand corner. Work across the entire row from selvage to selvage, always starting at left edges and changing colors when necessary. It is difficult to fill in colors later if you work one color at a time. When you are more experienced, you can skip around.

It is *very important* to have all the knots face in one direction, so always work with the unfinished portion of the canvas farthest away from you.

To make it easier to work on a large rug, sit at a table with the unfinished canvas weighted down on the table and the row you are working on at the edge of the table.

I keep a pile of cut wool of all the colors I need right on the canvas near the area on which I am working and pull each strand as I need it.

It is quicker than keeping the colors in separate piles in a bag somewhere.

Be sure to fill in every space on the canvas. A check of the back will reveal any skipped spaces.

If the canvas is resting on your lap, it is a good idea to slip a thin magazine or piece of cardboard under the canvas so that your hook will not catch onto anything as it goes through the canvas.

DESIGNS

Designs for latch hooked rugs should not have tiny details as they will get lost in the pile. Large, bold lines show up most effectively.

I prefer to do latch hooking from a graph pattern rather than painting on the canvas. Since the spaces on the canvas are geometric, it is more accurate to follow the design space for space. Also, as in needlepoint, you cannot get a perfect curve or circle; it must be done in graduated steps—one up, one over, etc. Following a graph, which clearly shows these steps, is easy and exact. Check the graphs in this book to see how a curved line is latched.

If you want to put the design right on the canvas, follow the directions for "Transferring Designs" in Chapter 1.

Try different pile heights for a sculptured effect.

The rug on page 92 was done with 1½-inch pieces, making a pile of ½ inch. This gives the finished rug a tighter look with less shagginess.

To get the effect of a rya, use pile 3½ to 4½ inches long and leave one or two rows unhooked between each row of knots. Two unhooked rows will let the pile fall into a real shag. You can combine two strands, each of a different color and length for an interesting variation.

SHEEP
(See photograph on p. 92)

A traditional lamb's tongue worked in monochromatic colors. Cut a tongue-shaped pattern from a stiff piece of cardboard. After you have decided on your rug size, allow a border of about 2 inches all around, then trace an odd number of tongues across the bottom row as shown in photograph. Start the second row by alternating tongues, making sure that each pattern is between two from the previous row. Start hooking by outlining each tongue with a dark color, then use 2 rows of a light or medium color, depending on what color the center will be. Each tongue will have 3 colors: the outline, 2 rows of the second color, and the rest filled in with the third. Make certain that you plan on one very light color to highlight the diamond pattern as shown.

TOY BLOCKS. Latch hooked rug mat designed and made by author. To enlarge to a larger rug size, do two stitches for every square on the graph.

FRAN. Latch hooked rug designed and made by **Professor Irwin Corey**. This design is also suitable for hooked and embroidered rugs. (See color plate 21)

Reverse side of FRAN. Pattern is clearer.

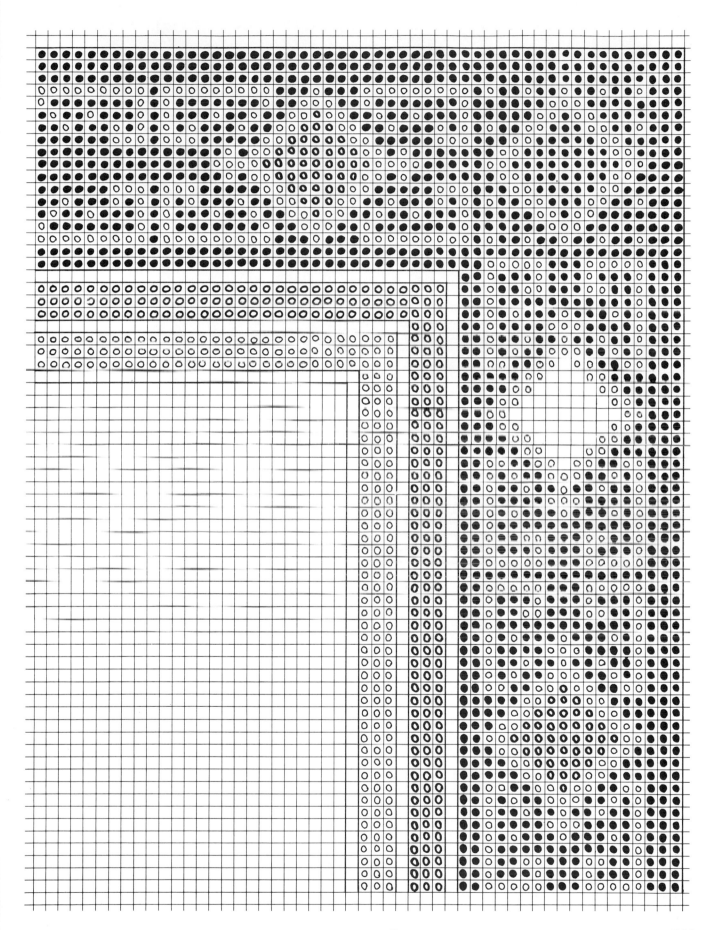

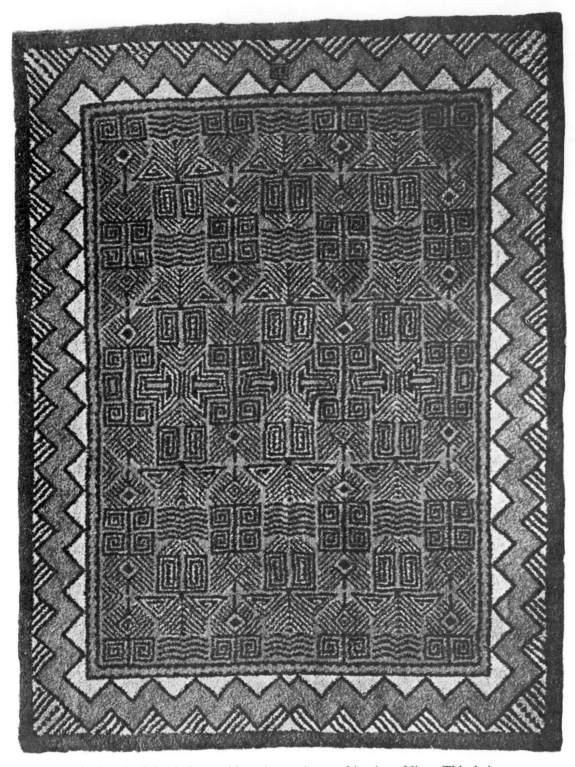

ATLANTIS. Antique latch hooked rug with an interesting combination of lines. This design can be used for hooked and embroidered rugs. From *Arts and Decoration,* 1924.

103

RENÉE. Latch hooked rug for a child's room designed by Bernard Glickman and made by Shirley Glickman. The pattern was hooked in pastel colors against a navy background.

104

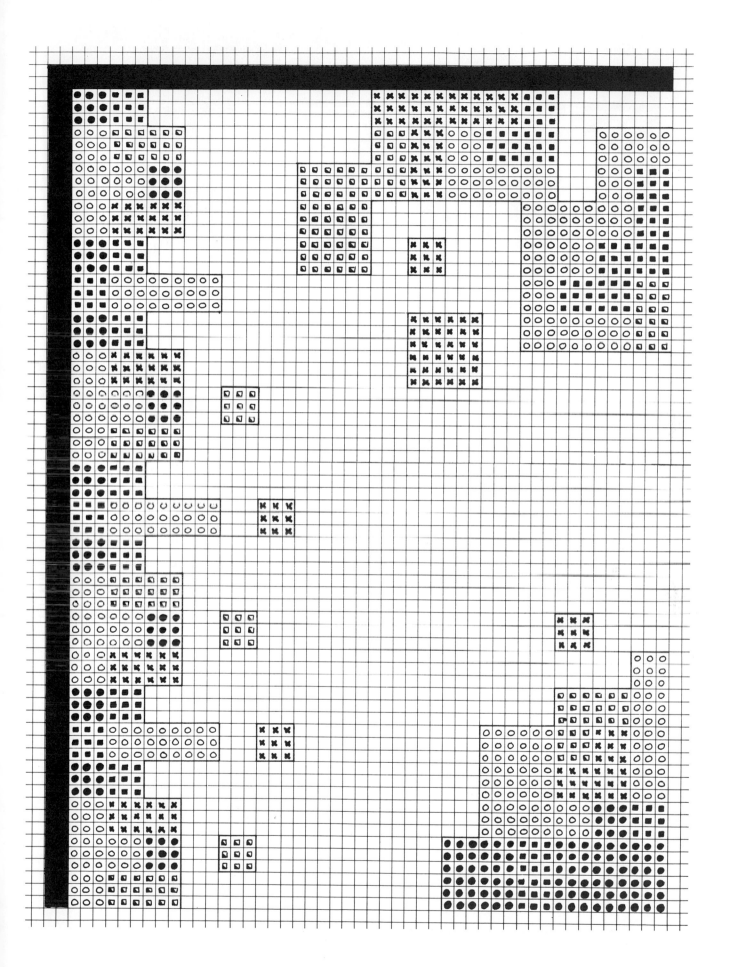

105

PATCHED SAMPLER. Needlepoint rug using continental, basketweave, and cross-stitches in eight shades of blue. Designed and made by Ruth Bushell Levin.

7 EMBROIDERED RUGS

INTRODUCTION

Smooth-faced rugs made of flat, embroidered stitches rather than pile are beautiful, enjoyable to make, and, because they use less yarn than pile rugs, are less costly. Many canvas-work stitches can be used for smooth-faced rugs, although I prefer not to use either vertical or horizontal stitches, as they do not cover the warp and weft of the canvas as well as slanted stitches.

EQUIPMENT

Canvas

There are essentially two types of canvas used for embroidered rugs: the mono, or single thread; and the penelope, or double-thread mesh. Either can be used satisfactorily.

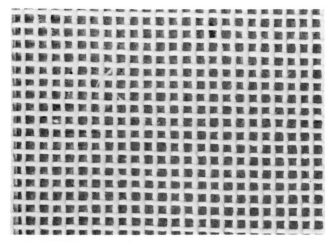

Mono canvas

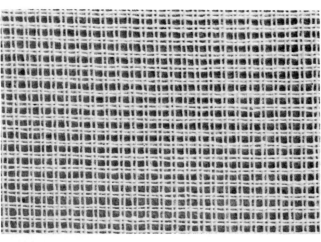

Penelope canvas

These canvases come in varying widths up to 54 inches. If you want to make a wider rug, see instructions for joining canvas on page 94. The size of the mesh ranges from 3 up to 20 holes to the inch. I use 5 to the inch for most of my embroidered rugs. I think anything larger is not durable enough and doesn't look as handsome. I have also used 10-to-the-inch canvas for rugs. These are, of course, lovely and wear well but take much more time. If you don't get bored working on the same project for a long time, try the smaller mesh; it is well worth the added time and work. The rugs on pages 122 (color plate 28) and 128 (color plate 29) were made on 10-to-the-inch canvas.

Yarn

I recommend using all-wool yarns for embroidered rugs, since they are available from many manufacturers in a wide range of colors. For smaller meshes I use a needlepoint yarn of three strands. The important thing to remember is that the yarn must cover the mesh and yet not be so thick that it looks cramped. When you have decided on the stitch and mesh size, try out various weights of yarn until you get one that works comfortably. You can double or triple thin yarn to get the desired thickness. This also enables you to get a mottled effect if you combine different colors.

The quantity of yarn depends on many factors: the stitch, the canvas, and the tension of your work. A good average rule for smooth-faced needlework rugs is about 6 ounces of yarn to a square foot of canvas. If you want to make frequent color changes, you will need more yarn. Always figure the amounts roughly and then buy more than your estimate.

Needles

The needles used for canvas work are made of steel, are blunt, and have long eyes. The size of the needle is determined by the thickness of the yarn and the size of the mesh you are using. As the size of the needle increases, the number decreases. For a 10-to-the-inch canvas I use a #18 needle. For a 5-to-the-inch mesh I use a #14 needle. Just make sure that the yarn goes through the eye of the needle easily and that the needle isn't so large that it distorts the mesh.

Scissors

It is important to have a pair of sharp, pointed scissors. The pointed end is useful if you have to rip, and the sharp edge won't leave a ragged edge on the yarn.

Masking Tape

Protect raw edges of the canvas with masking tape. This not only protects the canvas but also keeps the edge from catching and scratching.

STITCHES

The Continental

This simple stitch is used most frequently for needlepoint designs. Work is started at the top right-hand corner of the design (see illustration). For the first stitch, bring needle up at 1 and down at 2. For the second stitch, bring the needle up at 3 (from under the canvas) and down at 4, and for the third stitch, bring the needle up at 5 and down at 6. Keep repeating along the row. All odd numbers are down from front to back. Even numbers come up from back to front. For the second row, turn the canvas around and continue in the opposite direction.

If you are left-handed, turn diagram around and start at lower left-hand corner.

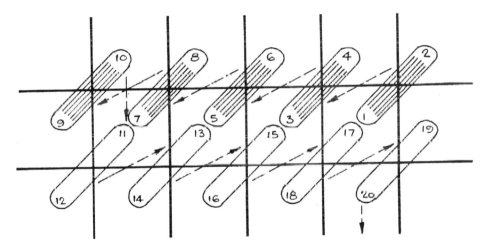

Continental stitch

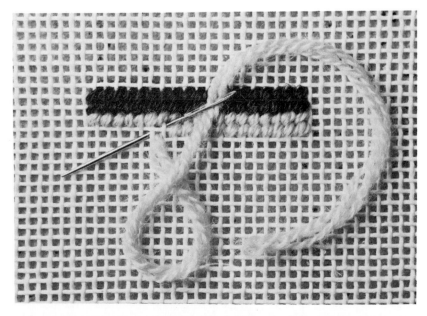

Basketweave

Basketweave is a good durable stitch for rugs because the back is woven and therefore heavier. It uses more yarn than the continental stitch but doesn't distort the shape of the canvas as much.

Always go up one diagonal row and down another. Two rows done in the same direction will cause a slight ridge that can be very noticeable in a large background area.

For the first stitch, bring the needle up at 1 and down at 2. For the second stitch, bring the needle up at 3 and down at 4, and for the third stitch, bring the needle up at 5 and down at 6. Keep going up one row and down another until you have filled in the area.

The odd numbers, 1, 3, 5, 7, etc., indicate that the needle comes up from back to front. The even numbers, 2, 4, 6, 8, etc., indicate that the needle goes down from front to back.

Keep in mind that all diagonal movements of the needle are on top on the finished surface, and that all horizontal and vertical movements of the needle are on the underside, or back of the canvas, except for the first stitch of a new row.

Always start from top right-hand corner. Left-handed people start at the lower left-hand corner.

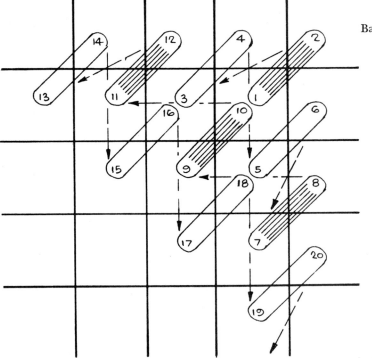

Basketweave stitch

Cross-Stitch

The old familiar cross-stitch is very effective when used for rugs. The double stitch adds strength to the rug and in certain designs will show up better than the continental stitch, which only goes in one direction. Animals on rug on page 134 (color plate 22) were done in cross-stitch.

You can work the cross-stitch two ways. Half of the stitch can be done across a row and completed as you go back across the row again, or you can complete each cross as you go. Either way, be careful that your top stitches always slant in the same direction.

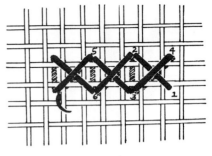

Cross-stitch

Long-Legged Cross-Stitch

I recommend this stitch for use between rows of rya knots. It is also a good edging stitch and can be used for background or borders on an embroidered rug.

Start and end each row with a small cross-stitch. Make sure that the first part of the cross is worked in the direction you are going—either left to right, right to left, up, or down. After the first stitch the long leg is worked over double the number of threads as the short leg. Go up at 1 and down at 2, up at 3 and down at 4, up at 1 and down at 5, up at 6 and down at 2, up at 3 and down at 7, up at 8, etc.

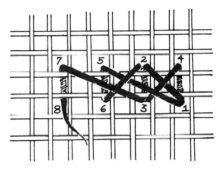

Long-legged cross-stitch

Rice Stitch

This is a large cross-stitch with crossed corners. It is a strong stitch but uses a large amount of yarn. If you use it in successive rows, you may want to put a backstitch in between each row to prevent the canvas from showing through. The rice stitch is lovely when combined with the long-legged cross-stitch in alternating rows. (You won't need the backstitch if you combine the two stitches.) It is a good stitch for background work or bands.

Notice that the large cross is worked over 3 holes.

Come up at 1 and down at 2, up at 3 and down at 4, up at 5 and down at 6, up at 7 and down at 5, up at 8 and down at 6, up at 7 and down at 8, and up at 3 to start the next large cross.

For variety you could do all the large crosses first and do the small crosses in a second color.

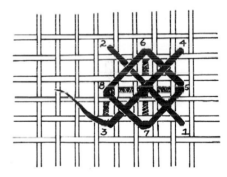

Rice stitch

Soumak or Knitting Stitch

This stitch is similar to the stitch found on old Caucasian Soumak rugs, which were woven on looms and had no pile. The Soumak stitch also looks like the stockinette stitch used in knitting. It is simple to do and is quite durable. A similar effect can be made by doing the continental stitch going in alternating diagonal directions every other row.

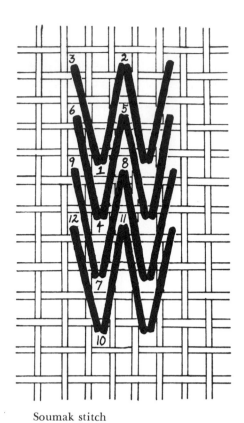

Soumak stitch

When you work the Soumak stitch, keep the selvages horizontal and the bottom of the V facing you.

Come up at 1 and down at 2, up at 3 and down at 1, up at 4 and down at 5, up at 6 and down at 4, etc. Always complete each V before going on to another.

Once you get into the swing of it, you will enjoy working this stitch. If you want to go in different directions rather than down as shown on the diagram, just move the needle one thread over in the direction in which you want to travel. Work the backstitch on the first and last rows and the edges to cover all the canvas.

Soumak stitch detail

Interlocking Gobelin Stitch

This is a quick, easy, and excellent stitch for borders or backgrounds. If you want to make an entire rug of a simple striped pattern, this is an excellent way to use up odd bits of yarn. Work the stitch across the width of your canvas from selvage to selvage. You are actually making one half of a cross-stitch done over one thread horizontally and two threads vertically. When you start each new row go down an extra hole and come up two threads vertically.

Up at 1 and down at 2, up at 3 and down at 4, up at 5 and down at 6, up at 7 and down at 8, up at 9 and down at 10, up at 11 and down at 12, up at 13 and down at 14, etc.

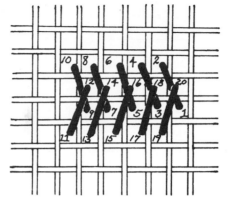

Interlocking gobelin stitch

Embroidered sampler. Stitches from top to bottom: interlocking gobelin stitch, rice stitch, interlocking gobelin stitch, cross stitch, Soumak stitch, long-legged cross-stitch, interlocking gobelin stitch.

DESIGNS

Most of the graphed designs used in this book are suitable for embroidered rugs. It is not necessary to copy the design onto the canvas. Actually, it is more accurate to work from a graph, as each box represents a single stitch. When you are using stitches other than basket-weave or continental (which use only one mesh), you will have to compensate for the additional width and height of the stitch. For example, a simple cross-stitch will use twice as many meshes. Because it may be difficult to translate a design to the larger stitches, I suggest them mainly for backgrounds, bands, or borders. Experiment before you begin work on your rug canvas. For additional designs see my book *The Needlepoint Workbook of Traditional Designs* (Hawthorn, 1973). In it you will find many beautiful ethnic designs, which you can use in unlimited combinations.

RUNNING BROOK. Needle-point rug inspired by Navaho motif using continental stitch. Designed and made by the author. (See color plate 23)

115

116

PRAYER RUG. Needlepoint rug using continental stitch. Designed by the author and made by Helen Tandler. (See color plate 24)

117

HARRY. Needlepoint rug using basketweave and continental stitches. Designed by the author and made by Sandra Choron. (See color plate 26)

CANTON. Needlepoint rug using
continental stitch. Designed by the
author and made by Lynne Scire.

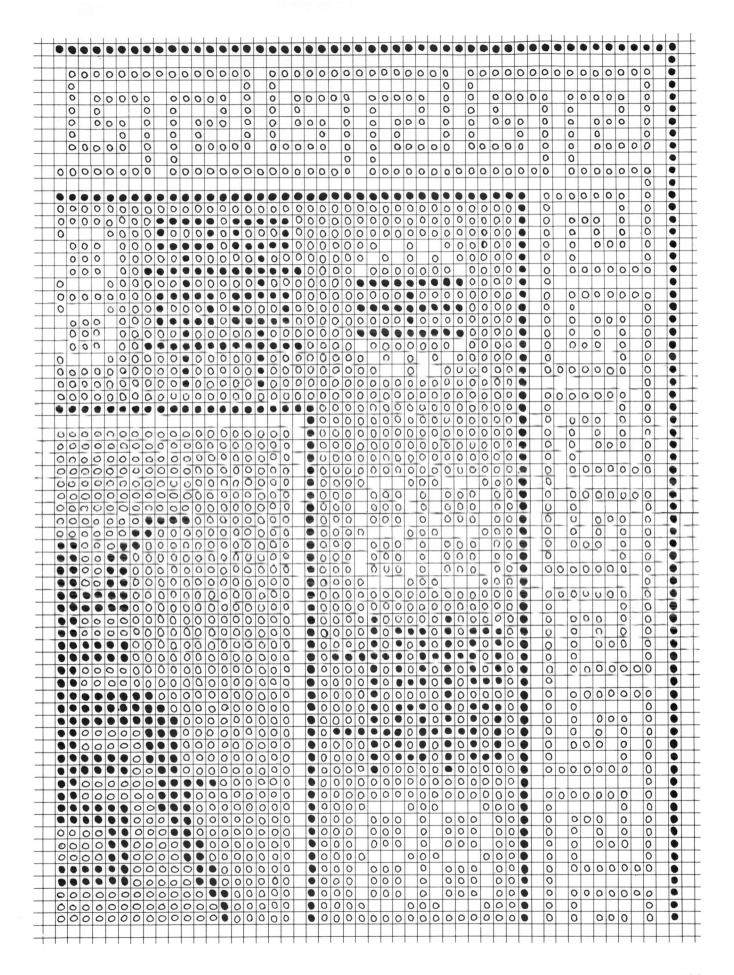

ORIENTAL BAZAAR. Needlepoint rug using continental and basketweave stitches. Designed by Sol Zaret and made by Minna Zaret. Graphs of details appear on the following three pages. (See color plate 28)

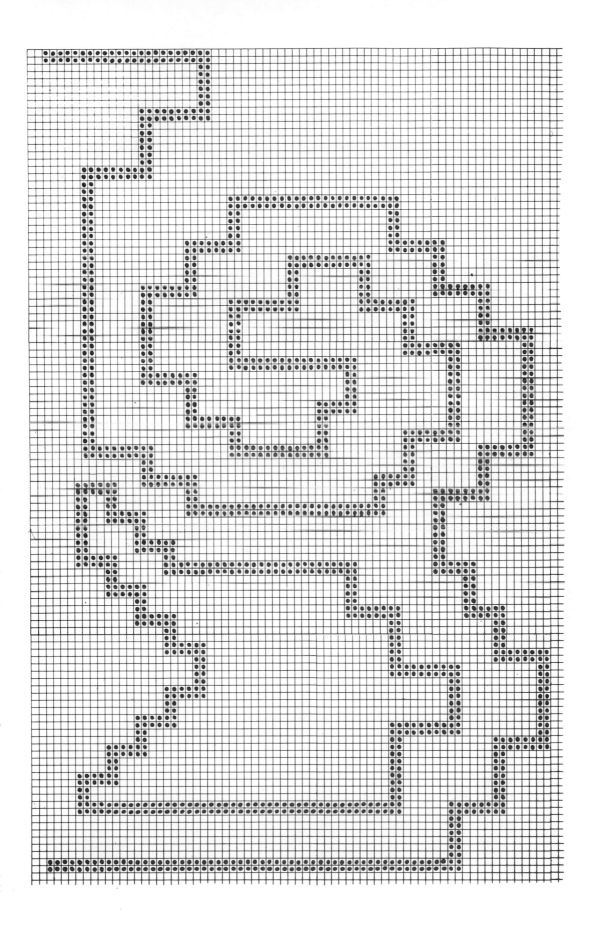

123

124

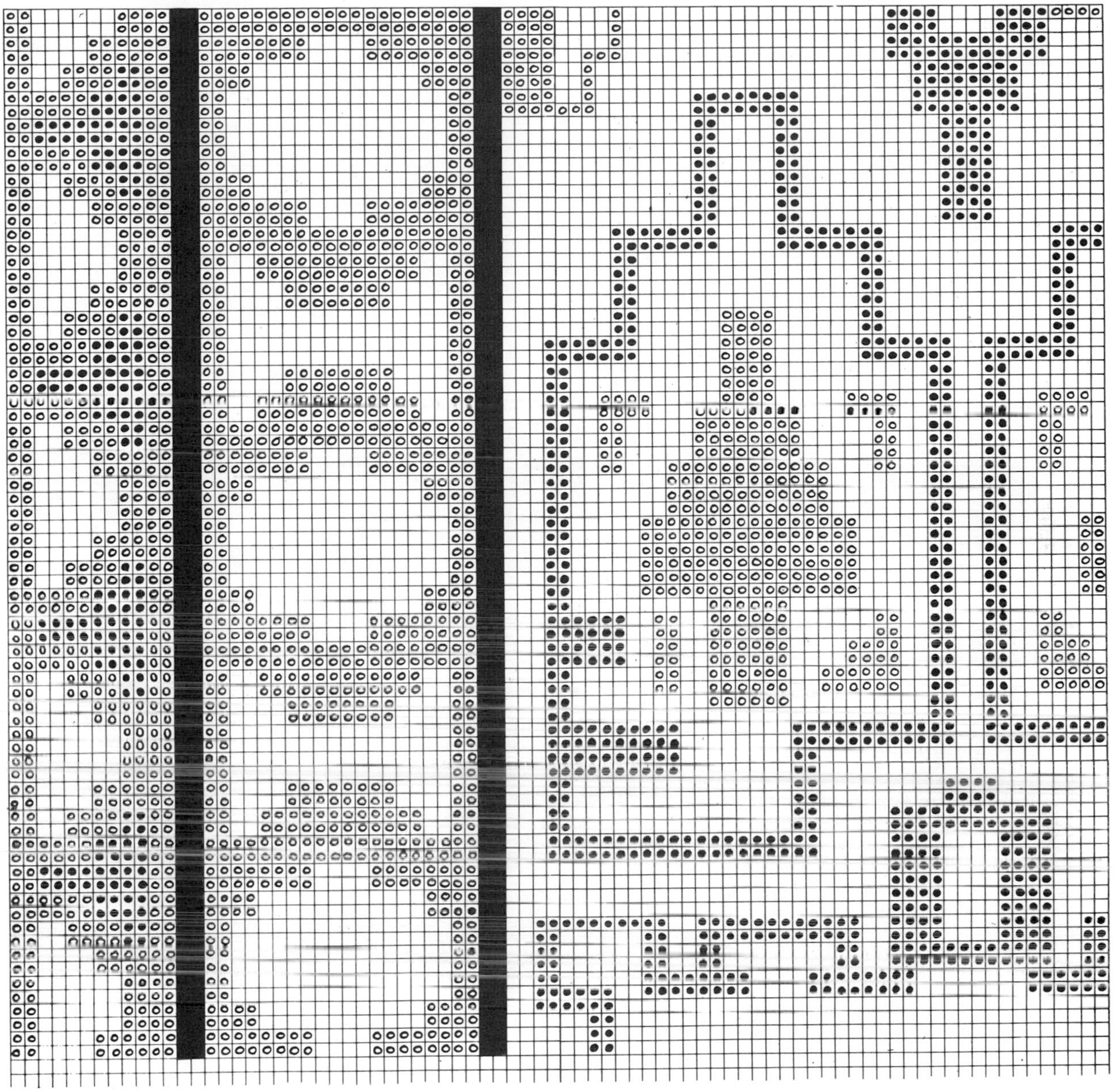

STEPPING STONES. Antique rug (unfinished) using Soumak stitch. Collection of Eunice Plesser. (See color plate 27)

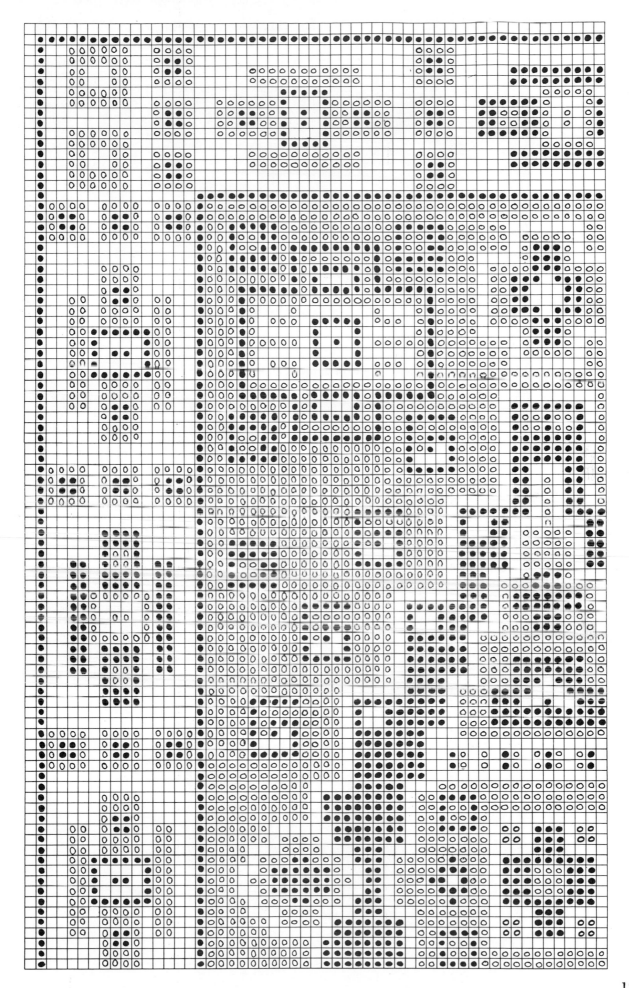

127

128

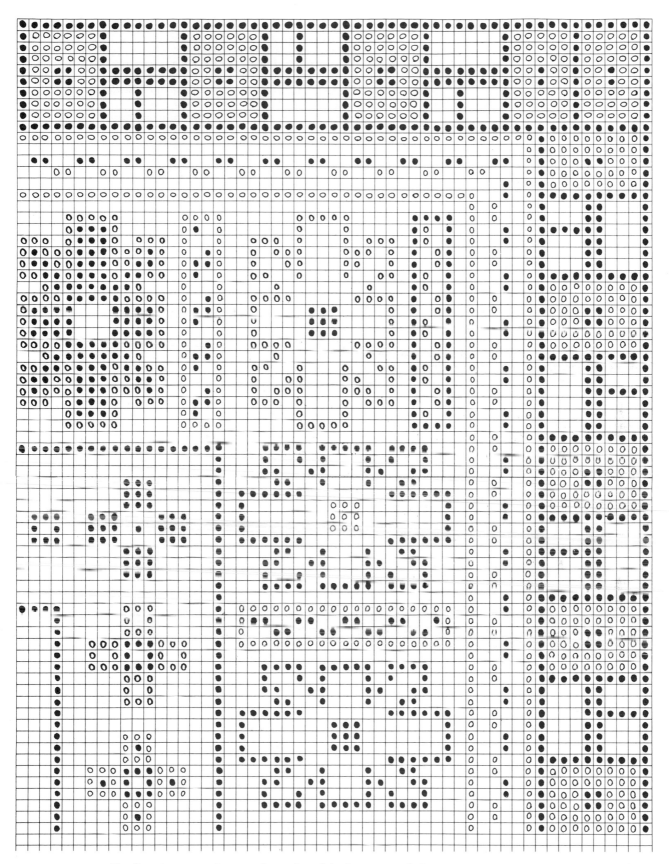

PERSIAN DELIGHT. Needlepoint rug using continental and basketweave stitches. Designed and made by the author. This rug was made on 10-to-the-inch canvas. Graphs of details appear on the following pages. (See color plate 29)

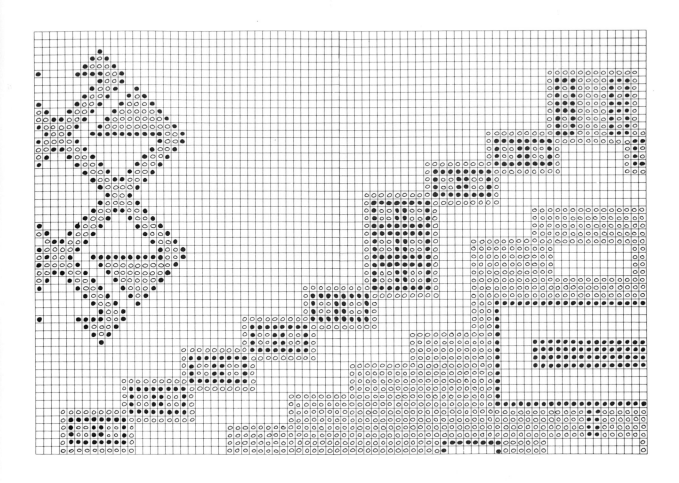

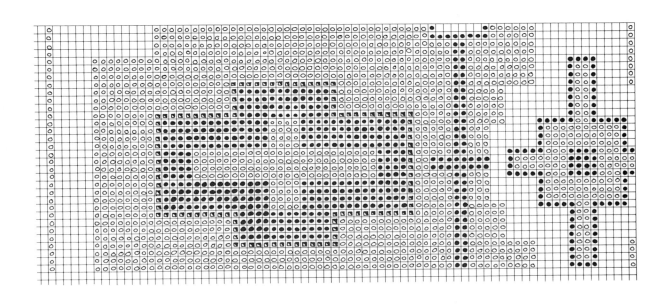

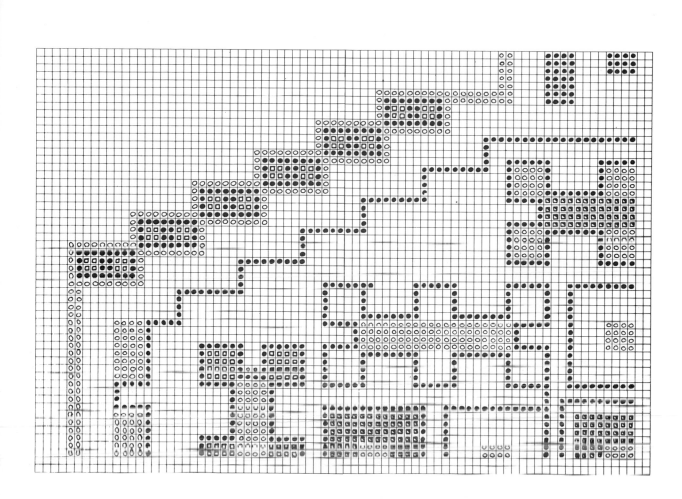

131

132

NAVAHO. Designed by the author and made by Irma and Ken Philmus.

134

CUBES WITH DOGS. Needlepoint rug using basketweave, continental, and cross-stitches. Designed and made by the author. (See color plate 22)

136

BOKARA. Needlepoint rug using continental and basketweave stitches. Designed by the author and made by Helen Tandler. To make this rug larger, increase each border and use more space between each center design. (See color plate 25)

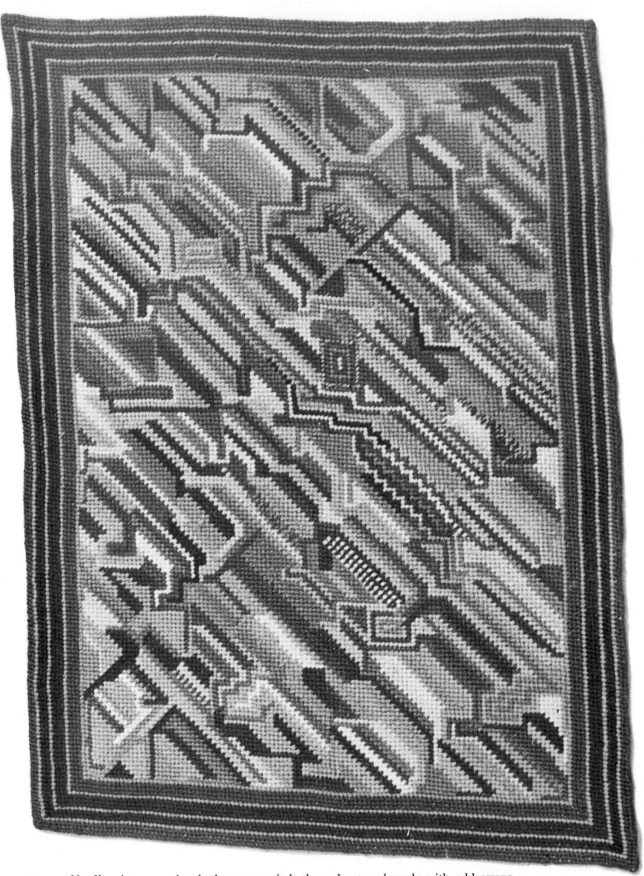

LIZZIE. Needlepoint rug using basketweave stitch throughout and made with odd scraps of leftover yarn. Start in top right-hand corner (leaving room for a border or two) and do basketweave stitch back and forth on the diagonal, ending colors in different places. Don't be afraid to try wild shapes with each color. Designed and made by Gladys Blum.

PAISLEY. Needlepoint rug using continental and basketweave stitches. Designed and made by Ruth Bushell Levin.

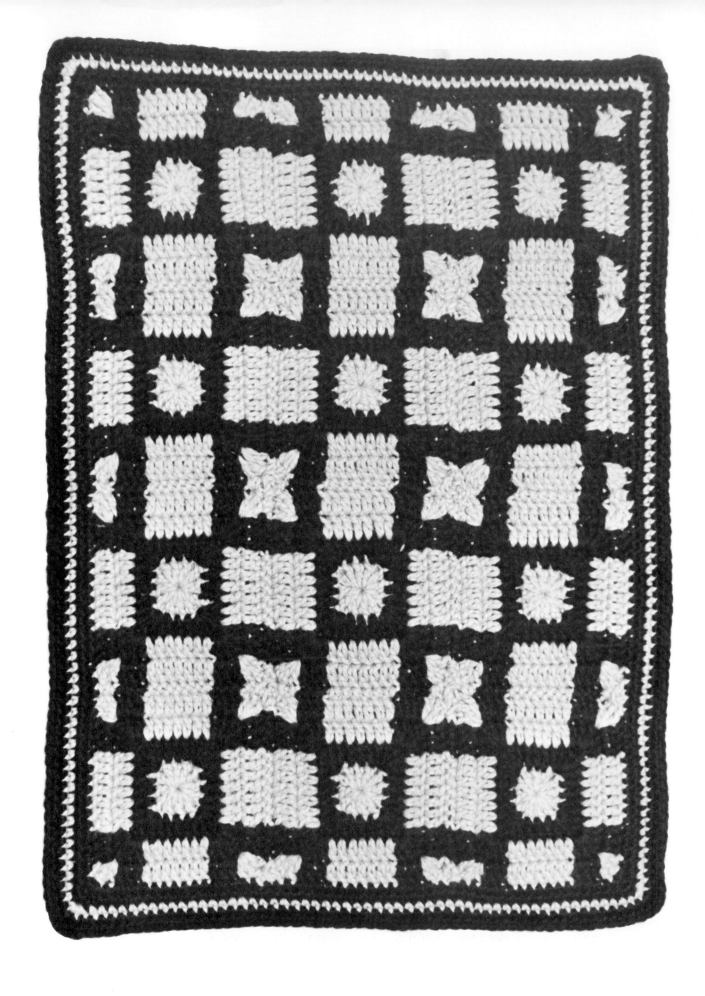

140

8 CROCHETED RUGS

HISTORY

Early crocheting was used mainly for lace-making. It slowly evolved into the versatile craft we know today.

My earliest recollections of childhood include visions of my mother with a crochet hook and thread in her hands. She made crocheted doilies for every lamp, as well as crocheted bedspreads and curtains or fabric curtains edged with crochet. My best handkerchiefs always had delicate crocheted edges. And scattered throughout the house were crocheted rugs.

The Encyclopedia of Victorian Needlework says that

> The word crochet is derived from the French *croches* or *croc* and old Danish *krooke,* a hook. This art was known in the sixteenth century but was then chiefly practiced in nunneries and was indifferently classed as nun's work.

Crocheting has many advantages. Not only is it easy to learn, but it is probably the fastest hand stitch known. It is resistant to wear, and when used for rugs has good body and can be made in large sizes without the restrictions knitting needles have. It does, however, require more yarn than knitting.

EQUIPMENT

Crochet Hooks

Crochet hooks are made of bone, aluminum, steel, plastic, or wood. Your own preference dictates your choice. The size of the hook (and the resulting number of stitches per inch) are matters of personal preference, although for heavier yarns you will want to use heavier hooks. The tension of your own work is also a factor in determining the size of the hook. Experiment with different size hooks after you have selected your yarn weight. See which feels best to you after you have crocheted a few rows with different size hooks.

Crocheting can be done with almost any type of threads (cotton, wool, synthetics, and jute of any weight) or even rag strips.

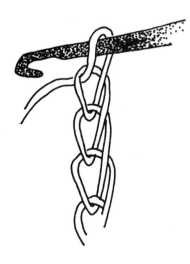

Chain stitch. Insert hook through loop. Catch the hook onto the unused yarn and draw through the loop, making a new loop. *(Drawings by Deborah Magid)*

STITCHES

The crocheted rugs I have selected are all simple to make and require a basic knowledge of crochet stitches: chain (ch), single crochet (sc), double crochet (dc), and slip stitch (sl st). Yarn over hook (YO) means to take up the unused thread with the hook.

To begin, hold the hook in your right hand as you would a pencil. Hold the yarn in your left hand wound over your forefinger and/or between your fourth and little finger to get the proper tension. Be careful not to hold the yarn too tightly or it will pull your stitches.

Chain Stitch (ch)

Make a slip knot at the end of the yarn leaving about 2 inches free. Insert hook through the loop. Catch the hook onto unused yarn and draw through the loop, making another loop. Continue for the number of stitches required. Keep the thumb and forefinger of your left hand close to the last chain as you work.

Single Crochet (sc)

After you have completed your first row of chain stitches, insert hook from the front under the two top threads of the second chain from the hook. With your hook, catch the yarn and draw through chain stitch (ch). You now have two loops on your hook. Yarn over hook (YO) and draw through both loops. You now have one loop on your hook.

Double Crochet (dc)

Yarn over (YO), insert hook into chain, and draw up a loop. YO again and pull through the first two loops on your hook. YO again and pull through the last two loops on your hook. You now have one loop on your hook.

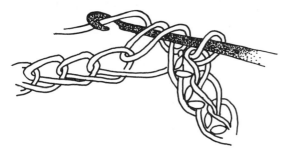

Single crochet stitch: Insert hook from the front under the two top threads of the second chain from the hook. Catch the yarn with the hook and draw through chain stitch.

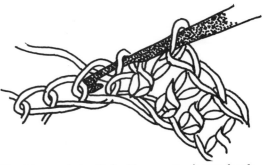

Double crochet stitch: Yarn over, insert hook into chain, and draw up a loop.

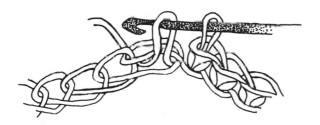

You now have two loops on your hook. Yarn over hook and draw through both loops.

Yarn over again and pull through first two loops on your chain.

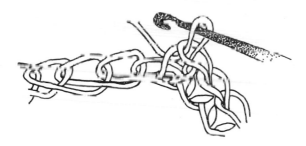

You now have one loop on your hook and are ready for the next stitch.
(*Drawings by Deborah Magid*)

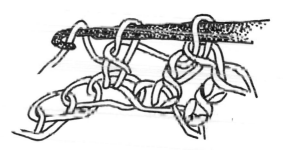

Yarn over again and pull through last two loops.

You wind up with one loop on your hook.
(*Drawings by Deborah Magid*)

Slip stitch: Insert hook, yarn over, and in one motion draw through stitch and loop on the hook. *(Drawing by Deborah Magid)*

Slip Stitch (sl st)

This stitch is used in joining a round or when an invisible stitch is required. It doesn't add to the height.

Insert hook as for sc. Yarn over and in one motion draw through stitch and loop on the hook.

Increase

Make two stitches in one stitch of the previous row. Each time you do this you increase one stitch.

Decrease

To decrease in a double crochet stitch (dc), yarn over, insert hook stitch and draw a loop through. Insert hook into the next stitch and draw a loop through. Yarn over and draw through the three loops on the hook.

Or just skip a stitch.

To decrease in a double crochet stitch (dc), yarn over, insert hook into the next stitch, and draw a loop through—YO and draw a loop through. Insert into next stitch, YO, and pull up a loop. YO and draw through all five loops.

You have now worked two stitches together, and there is one less stitch in the row.

DESIGNS

OHIO OVAL

See color plate 30.

Materials:

1 main color rug yarn

1 crochet hook, size K

Stitches:

Rug is worked in sc and puff stitch.

Puff stitch: yarn over needle, insert in stitch (st) and pull loop up to the length of a dc, yarn over needle, insert in same stitch, and pull loop up to the same length, yarn over and pull through all loops on needle but one, yarn over and pull through two loops.

Notes:

1. Single crochet may be worked round and round without joining. Even off the end before puff st by one or two sl sts.

2. Puff st rows begin with ch 3 and end with a slip st into the top of the ch 3.

3. A marker at each end will help to keep increases balanced evenly.

Chain 34, 2 sc in 2nd chain from hook, 1 sc in each chain, 3 sc in end stitch, 1 sc in each st on opposite side of chain, 1 sc in starting chain.

Work 7 rounds of sc increasing 3 sts each end of every round. Increases should be spaced evenly at each end and located to keep the work flat.

Work 2 rounds of puff st continuing to increase 3 sts each end of every row.

Work 7 rounds of sc increasing 4 sts each end of every row.

Work 2 rounds of puff st (no increases unless necessary to keep work flat).

Work 6 rounds of sc increasing 4 sts each end of every row.

Work 2 rows of puff sts (no increases unless necessary to keep work flat), join, end off.

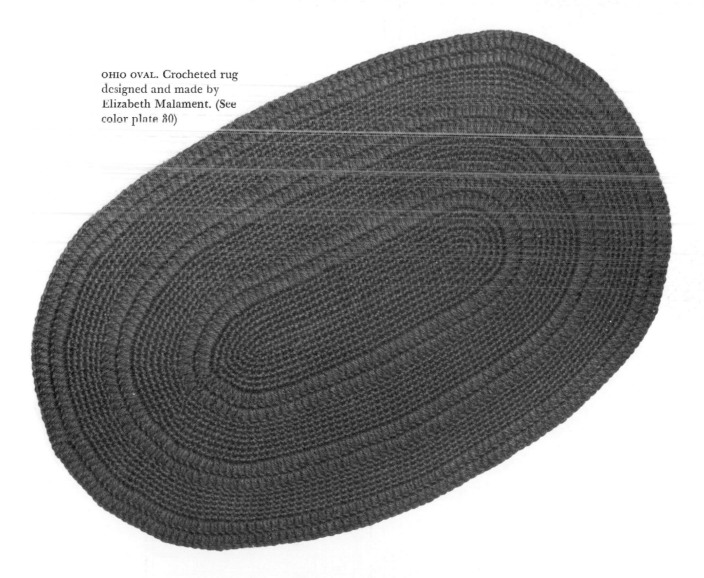

OHIO OVAL. Crocheted rug designed and made by Elizabeth Malament. (See color plate 80)

LONDON SQUARES. Crocheted rug designed and made by Elizabeth Malament. (See color plate 31)

146

See color plate 31.

Materials:

    Rug yarn: Color A

           Color B

           (1 double skein will make 6 squares)

    1 crochet hook, size K

    Each square is approximately 8 inches.

Notes:

1. When changing colors, hold back the last 2 sts of the original color, and pull through the new color. Carry previous color in back, at bottom, working over it.

2. All corners are made with 5 dc. To square them off, make the center d c looser than the others.

3. Beginning with round 2 start all rounds at a corner. Do half the corner at the beginning of the row (ch 3 loosely and 2 d c in the joining st); finish the first corner at the end of the round by doing 2 more dc in the same st as the ch 3.

Round 1: With color A, chain 5. In 2nd ch from start make 2 dc, ch 1, (3 dc, ch 1) 3 times; join with slip st in 3rd ch of chain 3; break off.

Round 2: Attach color B to a corner. Ch 3 loosely and 2 dc in corner, chain 1 dc in each of next 3 dc; (5 dc in corner in chain, dc in next 3 dc), 3 times, 2 dc in original joining st. Join to top of ch 3.

Round 3: With color B, chain 3 loosely and 2 dc in joining st. *Drop color B, attach color A, 1 dc over ea. of 7 dc of previous row. Drop color A. Attach color B, 5 dc in center dc of corner of previous row. Repeat from * 2 more times. End with 7 dc in color A and 2 dc in color B. Join, drop color B.

Round 4: With color A ch 3 loosely and 1 dc in joining st. Drop color A. With color B, 1 dc in same st, and *1 dc in ea. of next 2 sts; drop color B. With color A, 7 dc, one over ea. dc in color A of previous row. Drop color A. With color B, 1 dc in each next 3 sts; drop color B. Make corner as follows: 3 dc in color A in same st as last dc in color B, drop color A; 1 dc in color B in same st. Repeat from * ending row with 1 dc in color A in same st as last dc in color B and slip st to ch 3 of the beginning of the round. Break off.

Sew together.

JOHANNESBURG. Crocheted rug made of jute thread by Elizabeth Malament.

JOHANNESBURG

Materials:

    Rug yarn: Main color (MC)

             Color A

             Color B

    1 crochet hook, size K

Notes:

    1. When changing colors, always draw new color through last two loops of the stitch.

2. Always carry unused colors across back of work and work new color over these threads.

3. Each row begins with chain 3 which counts as the first d c of the row; each row ends with a slip stitch in the top chain of the beginning chain 3. The beginning chain 3 is done loosely; the joining slip stitch may require the new color to be drawn through the two loops.

Stitches:

Row 1: Single crochet; all the rest, double crochet worked into the back loops of the preceding row.

Round 1: With MC ch 4, join with slip stitch, 12 sc in circle, join with sl st.

Rocnd 2: Ch 3, 2 dc in back loop of each st (24 dc), join.

Round 3: Ch 3, increase 16 sts evenly around the row (40 dc), join.

Round 4: Repeat round 3 (56 dc).

Round 5: Repeat rounds 3 and 4 (72 dc).

Round 6: Repeat rounds 3, 4, 5 (88 dc); drop MC; attach color A.

Round 7: With color A, ch 3 work dc around, increasing 18 st evenly (106 dc), join.

Round 8: With color A ch 3, 2 more dc in next 2 sts, drop A, *with color B work 12 dc over 10 of the previous row (an increase of 2, evenly spaced), 4 dc in color A, 12 color B over 10 (an increase of 2 evenly spaced), 3 color A. Repeat from * two more times; end with 12 color B (over 10), 4 color A, 12 color B.

Round 9: With color A, ch 3, 2 more dc, *on 12 color B of previous row work 3 color B, 7 M C, 3 color B; 1 color A on top of each A of previous row. Repeat from * to end of row, join, drop color A.

Round 10: With color B, ch 3, 3 more dc over the 2 color A of round 9, *15 color B over the next 13 of round 9, drop color B. With color A 4 dc, one in each color A of round 9, drop color A. With color B, 15 dc over 13 of round 9, 4 more color B over 4 color A of round 9. Repeat from * two more times; end with 15 color B over 13, 4 color A over 4 color A, 15 color B over 13, join, drop color B.

Round 11: With color A, ch 3, 3 dc over B of round 10, *3 color B over B, 13 color A over 12 B, 4 color A over A, 13 color A over 12 B, 3 color B, 4 color A. Repeat from * two more times, end with 13 color A over 12 color B, 4 color A over A, 13 A over 12 B, 3 B over 3 B, join, drop color B.

Round 12: With color A, ch 3, 3 more dc over A of round 11, *37 color B over 36 of round 11, 4 color A over color A. Repeat from * two more times, end with 37 color B over 36, join, drop color B.

Round 13: With color A, dc around increasing 16 sts evenly spaced to keep work flat, join, break off.

TUNISIAN CHECKERBOARD.
Crocheted rug with fringe
designed and made by
Elizabeth Malament.

TUNISIAN CHECKERBOARD

Materials:

Rug yarn: Light color A

             Dark color B

1 afghan needle (a long hooked needle of uniform diameter with a knob at the end), size 10.

Stitch:

Tunisian Simple—Chain required length

Row 1: Insert hook in second chain from hook, *wrap yarn around needle hook (wrh), draw through a loop, insert hook into next st, repeat from * leaving all loops on the hook. *Do not turn the work.*

Row 2: Wrh draw through a loop, *wrh, draw through 2 loops, repeat from * to end of row. One loop is left on hook.

Row 3: Insert the hook under the vertical thread from right to left and drawing a loop under the vertical thread. Repeat to end of row.

Tunisian Purl—Chain required length

Row 4: Repeat row 2.

Repeat rows 3 and 4.

Row 5: *First st as in Tunisian simple, 2nd st is purled by keeping the thread in front of the needle when picking up stitch. Repeat from *.

Row 6: Same as Tunisian simple.

Row 7: *Purl 1 st with thread forward, 1 Tunisian simple, repeat from *.

Row 8: Same as row 2.

Repeat rows 1–4, always reversing the order of Tunisian simple and purl stitches.

Notes:

Tunisian purl is easier to do if the thread is held down and forward with the left thumb.

When changing from one color to another and from Tunisian simple to purl, a neater checkerboard effect is achieved if the whole first row of the purl square is done in Tunisian simple, i.e., start the purl stitch on row 3 instead of row 1.

Rug is worked in 3 stripes of 6 squares in each. Increase size as desired.

Start with color A and purled Tunisian stitch. After a 6-inch square is completed, tie in color B yarn, and work 6 inches in Tunisian simple. Repeat until there are 3 color A and 2 color B squares. The center stripe starts and ends with color B squares of Tunisian simple.

To finish: Sew stripes together to form checkerboard pattern. Single crochet around the rug doing 3 sc in each corner. Fringe.

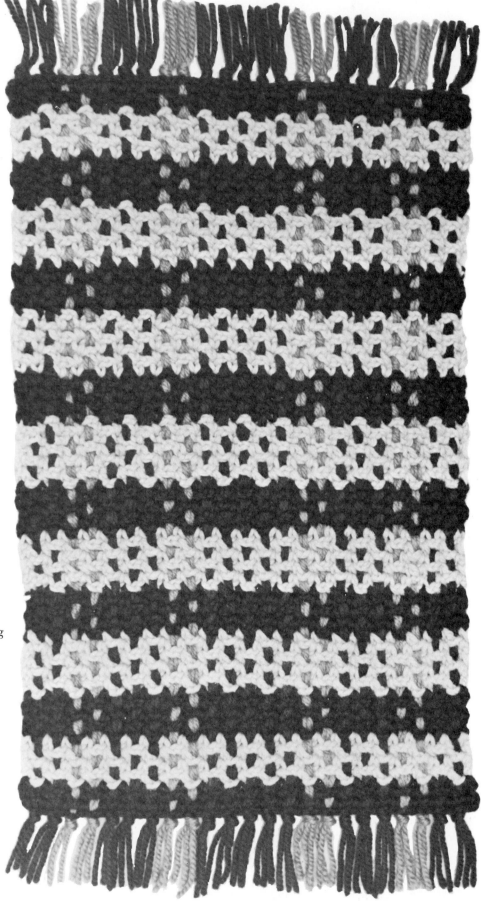

OLD MAINE. Crocheted rug with fringe designed and made by Elizabeth Malament.

Materials:

    Rug yarn: Light color A

               Dark color B

               Small amounts of as many other colors as desired for weaving

    1 crochet hook, size 11

    1 heavy blunt tapestry needle

Background stitch consists of squares which can be worked in sc, ch 1, sc; or in dc, ch 1, dc; or in tr, ch 1, sc depending on how firm a background is desired. The rug shown is done in sc, ch 1, sc squares for maximum firmness. Background may be done in one color, or in stripes of as many colors as desired. The rug shown was done in two colors, 5 rows of light and 4 rows of dark, repeated for desired length.

Chain desired width.

Row 1: *Sc in second ch from hook, ch 1, repeat from *.

Row 2: Ch 1, sc in last sc of previous row, *ch 1, sc over sc of previous row, repeat from *.

Repeat row 2 for desired length, making sure that there are the same number of squares in each row.

Vertical woven strands are added when the background is complete. Use 3 strands of yarn in desired color(s) threaded into a heavy, blunt tapestry darning needle. Weave *under* and *over* the chain 1 bar which separates the stitches. Next row weave *over* and *under* the chain 1 bar. (You are alternating the over and under in each row.)

Leave a good length of weaving threads at either end (about 5–6 inches each end), and knot for fringe.

GRANDMA'S DOILY. Crocheted rug in the shape of a doily or hexagon. Designed and made by Elizabeth Malament.

154

Materials:

    Rug yarn: Light color A

               Dark color B

    1 crochet hook, size K

Stitches:

    Double crochet and raised double crochet for spokes.

    Raised dc is done on row 2 and subsequent rows, never on the first row.

    Raised dc: Yarn around hook as for regular dc, insert hook in row below, from front to back between two stitches, bring hook up from back to front in next space, complete as for regular dc. In subsequent rows, raised dc stitches are always done over previous ones to form spokes.

Chain 3, join with sl st to form circle.

Round 1: Ch 3 (to count as dc), 11 dc in circle, join with sl st.

Round 2: Ch 3, 2 dc in joining st *a raised dc around next dc of previous row, 3 dc in next st, repeat from * ending with the 6th raised dc, join, drop light yarn.

Round 3: Attach dark yarn just before the raised dc, ch 3 *raised dc over previous raised dc, 2 dc in next st., 1 dc in each of next 3 dc, repeat from *, join. (There will be 6 spokes with 5 dc between raised dcs.)

Round 4: Attach light-colored yarn just before raised dc. Chain 3 * raised dc over previous raised dc, 2 dc in next st, 1 dc in each of next dcs up to the raised st, repeat from * to end of round, join.

Continue in this way, alternating 2 or 3 rows of light and 1 row of dark. Keep raised dc stitches in straight rows. Increase 12 sts each row, 2 in each section of the hexagon. Work to desired size.

Shell edging: Join dark yarn, sc *ch 2, 3 dc in same st as sc, skip 2 sts, sc in 3rd st, sc in next st, repeat from *.

Crocheted square with circle in it

Crocheted square

156

Materials:

    Rug yarn: Light color A

             Dark color B

    1 crochet hook, size K

Stitches:

    sc for squares

    dc and raised dc for spokes

Raised dc:

Yarn around hook as for regular dc, insert hook in row below, from front to back between two stitches, bring hook up from back to front in next space, complete as for regular dc. In subsequent rows, raised dc stitches are always done over previous ones to form spokes.

Ch 3, join with sl st to form circle.

Round 1: Ch 3 (to count as dc), 11 dc in circle. Join with sl st in top of starting ch.

Round 2: Ch 3, 1 dc and 1 raised dc in each of the 12 sts. There will be 12 spokes with 1 dc between spokes, 24 sts in all. Join with sl st into top of ch 3.

Round 3: Ch 3, *2 dc in next st, 1 raised dc under spoke of previous row. Repeat from *. There will be 36 sts in all, 12 spokes and 2 dc between spokes. Fasten off color A. Attach color B.

Round 4: Ch 1, 4 sc in same st, *sc in next 8 sts, 5 sc in next st. Repeat from * twice, sc in next 8 sts, sl st in 1st st. You now have 4 corners. Now work all sc in back loop only.

Round 5: Ch 1, 3 sc in next st, *12 sc to next corner, 3 sc in corner. Repeat from * to end of row, sl st in ch 1.

Round 6: Same as row 2, but 14 sts between corners. Fasten off.

Solid Square:

All stitches are sc and are worked in back loop.

Row 1: Ch 2, 12 sc in first ch, sl st in 1st st.

Row 2: Ch 1, *3 sc in same st (corner), sc in next 2 sts. Repeat from * to end of round, sl st in first st of first corner.

Rows 3 to 8: Continue in same manner, making a 3 sc corner in center of each corner, increasing the number of sts between corners by 2 until there are 14 st between corners. Fasten off

Finishing:

Sew squares together from the back, picking up only the back half of each sc.

Arrange squares as shown here or try a checkerboard.

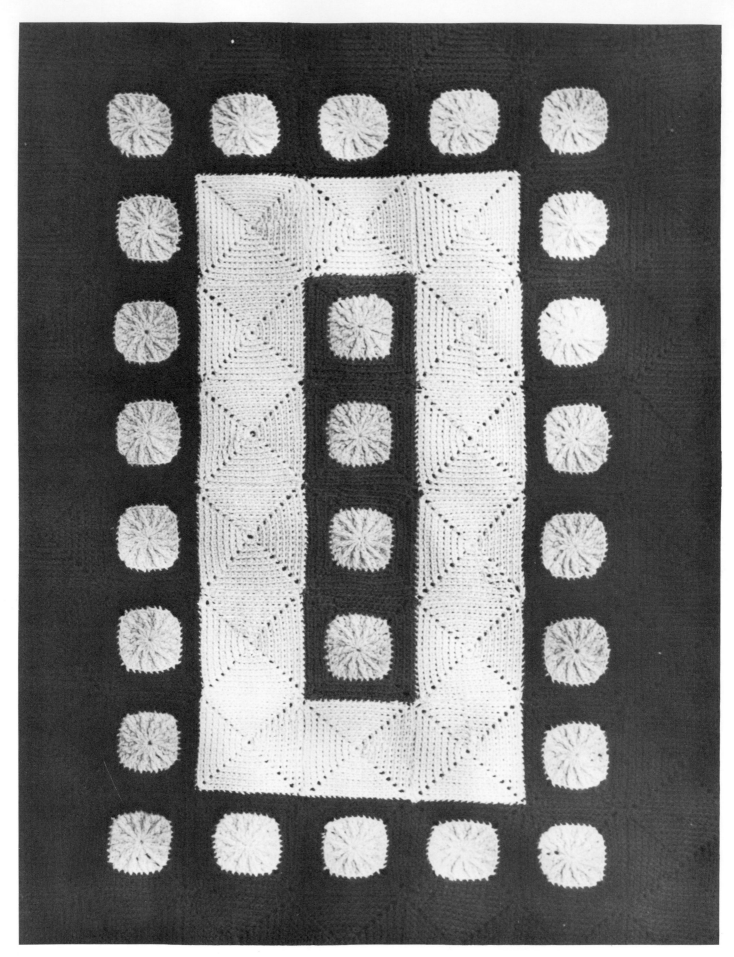

CIRCLE IN THE SQUARE. Crocheted rug made of spoked and solid squares. Designed and made by Doris Berger.

Single crochet used as background for pile. Two different piles are shown. They were added with a needle and hand-knotted.

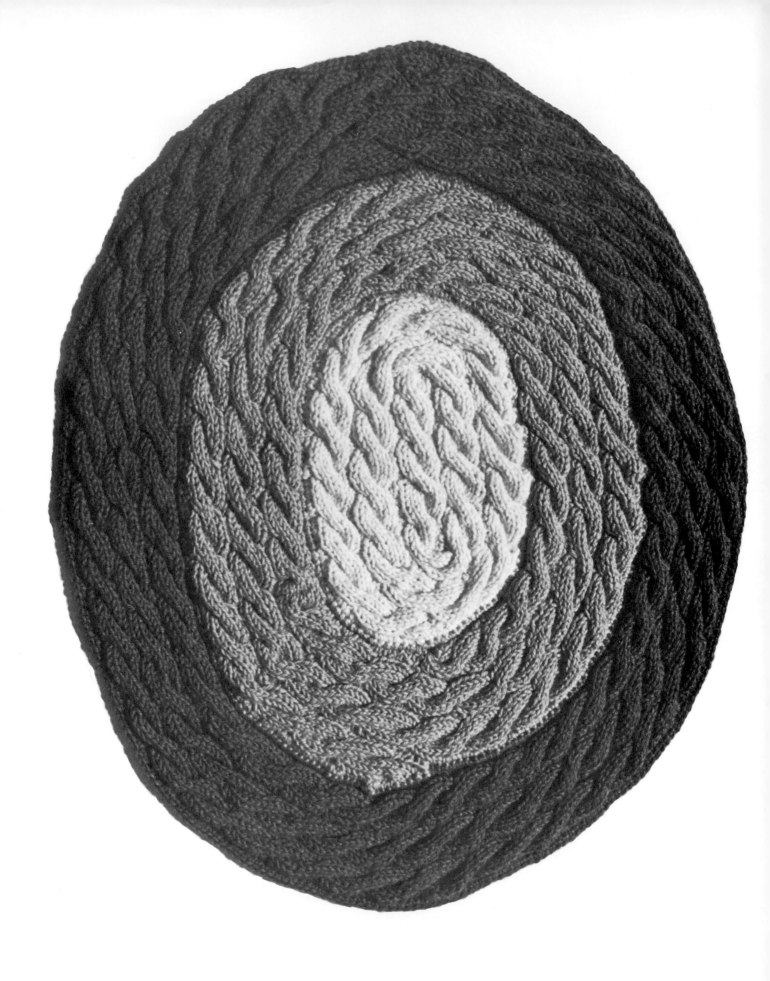

9 KNITTED RUGS

HISTORY

Knitting, according to information unearthed by anthropologists and historians, is an ancient craft. There are evidences of knitting in prehistoric Peru. Spaniards and Italians were known to knit before the English, yet the first knit stockings were made in England during the reign of Queen Elizabeth I. The word *knit* is derived from the Anglo-Saxon *Cnittan* and means threads woven by hand. *The Encyclopedia of Victorian Needlework* claims that knitting was first introduced to the Shetland Isles when the Spanish Armada was dispersed and the ship belonging to the Duke of Medina-Sidonia was wrecked at Fair Isle. The rescued sailors taught knitting to the inhabitants, who in turn introduced it to Scotland and England. Children were taught knitting at an early age, most often before they could read. Knitting remained a popular and useful craft until knitting mills started to mass produce items. However, knitting never has lost its popularity as a hobby and it is enjoying greater popularity today.

Knitted rugs are economical. They use less yarn than crocheted rugs, are durable, and don't require backing. There are some disadvantages, however. Knitted rugs can get very heavy on your knitting needles, thus making large knitted rugs impractical to handle. For this reason, if you plan to knit a very large rug, do it in strips or squares that you will later sew together. Always avoid lacy stitches, which will not give enough body to your rug and could create a hazard for women's heels.

PROCEDURES

Knitting should be done loosely enough for the needles to pass easily through the stitches, but not so loosely that the work sags. To start, you must cast on the number of stitches required. It is helpful

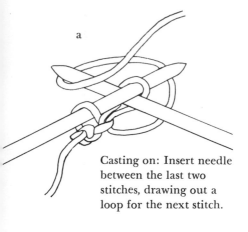

a

Casting on: Insert needle between the last two stitches, drawing out a loop for the next stitch.

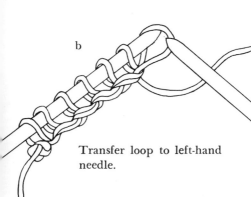

b

Transfer loop to left-hand needle.

to do a practice piece in order to gauge the number of stitches and rows you are making to the inch. It will vary with the size of the needle, thickness of the yarn, and yarn tension.

Casting On

Make a slip knot and pull the wool up through the loop onto the knitting needle. This forms the first stitch. Transfer the needle to the left hand. Insert right-hand needle through this stitch, draw another loop through, and place it on the left-hand needle. Add more stitches by inserting needle point between the last two stitches, drawing out a loop for the next stitch, and placing it on left-hand needle. Continue in this way until the required number of stitches is cast on. This method will give the work a double edge that stands up to hard wear.

To Knit (k)

Hold cast-on stitches in left hand between the first finger and thumb. Insert right-hand needle through the stitch to the back of the work. Wind the wool over the needle and draw a loop through the stitch onto the right-hand needle, at the same time dropping the stitch off the left-hand needle.

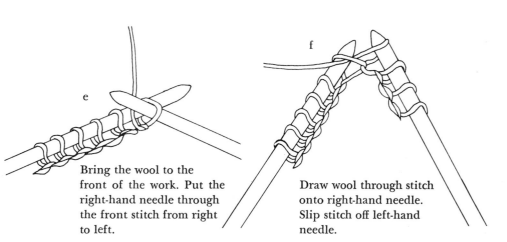

c

Insert right-hand needle through the front stitch to the back. Wind wool over needle.

e

Bring the wool to the front of the work. Put the right-hand needle through the front stitch from right to left.

f

Draw wool through stitch onto right-hand needle. Slip stitch off left-hand needle.

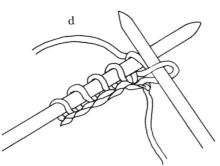

d

Draw a loop through the stitch onto the right-hand needle. Slip stitch off left-hand needle.

To Purl (p)

Hold hands as for knit stitch. Bring the wool to the front of the work. Put the right needle through the front stitch from right to left. Draw yarn through the stitch and onto the right-hand needle, at the same time dropping the stitch off the left-hand needle.

To Decrease

Slip the stitch to be decreased from the left-hand needle to the right-hand needle (without working through it in any way), work the next stitch as instructed in pattern, then use the point of the left-hand needle to lift the slipped stitch over the worked sitch and off the needle.

Another method of decreasing is to knit two stitches together as one.

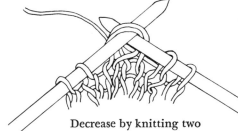

Decrease by knitting two stitches as one.

To Increase

In plain knitting, pass the wool to the front of the work through the needles and back again over the needles. In purl knitting, when the wool is already at the front, pass it over the right-hand needle and right around it, so that it comes out at the front. This will make a new stitch when worked off on the next row.

Slip Stitch

This stitch is used to make a hole or open stitch. Take a stitch off the left needle, slip it to the right needle without securing it in any way. The size of each hole is determined by the number of "overs" put around the needle. These open parts can be made in the work without increasing the number of stitches on the needles by knitting two together instead of one to make up for the slipped stitch.

To Bind Off

Work two stitches. With point of the left-hand needle lift the first stitch on the right-hand needle over the last one. Work one more stitch and continue lifting stitches off the needle in the same way until only one stitch remains on the right-hand needle. Draw thread through this loop and fasten off.

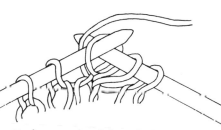

To increase in plain knitting, pass the wool to the front of the work through the needles and back again over the needles. In purl knitting, when the thread is already at the front, pass it over the right-hand needle and right around it, so that it comes out at the front.

DESIGNS

NANTUCKET CABLE

Materials:

One color rug yarn

1 pair knitting needles, size 11

1 double-pointed needle for cable

Notes:

1. The rug is made in strips. The width can be increased easily by adding more border stitches; length is optional.

2. The two side panels are identical except that the positions of the wide border and the cables are reversed.

3. Cable twists are done every four rows on alternate strips.

Stitches:

Borders are done in seed stitch: k 1, p 1 across; reverse k 1, p 1 on next and all subsequent rows.

Cable is done on 4 stitches. Slip 2 stitches to double-pointed needle and hold in back, k 2, k 2 from double-pointed needle.

Center panel: 27 stitches
Rows 1–4: K 1, p 1, repeat across.
Row 5: (K 1, p 1) 2 times, (k 4, p 1) 4 times, k 1, p 1, k 1.
Row 6: (K 1, p 1) 2 times, (p 4, k 1) 4 times, k 1, p 1, k 1.
Row 7: (K 1, p 1) 2 times, (k 4, p 1, cable on next 4, p 1) 2 times, k 1, p 1, k 1.
Row 8: Repeat row 6.
Row 9: Repeat row 5.
Row 10: Repeat row 6.
Row 11: (K 1, p 1) 2 times, (cable on next 4, p 1, k 4, p 1) 2 times, k 1, p 1, k 1.
Row 12: Repeat row 6.
Row 13: Repeat row 5.
Row 14: Repeat row 6.
Row 15: Repeat row 7.
Repeat rows 8–15 until piece measures desired size. Repeat row 6 once, row 5 once, then rows 1–3. Bind off in pattern.

Right side panel: 25 stitches
Rows 1–4: K 1, p 1, repeat across.
Row 5: (K 1, p 1) 6 times, (k 4, p 1) 2 times, k 1, p 1, k 1.
Row 6: K 1, p 1, k 1, (k 1, p 4) 2 times, (k 1, p 1) 6 times.
Row 7: (K 1, p 1) 6 times, k 4, p 1, cable on next 4, (p 1, k 1) 2 times.
Row 8: Repeat row 6.
Row 9: Repeat row 5.
Row 10: Repeat row 6.
Row 11: (K 1, p 1) 6 times, cable on next 4, p 1, k 4, (p 1, k 1) 2 times.
Row 12: Repeat row 6.
Row 13: Repeat row 5.
Row 14: Repeat row 6.
Row 15: Repeat row 7.
Repeat rows 8–15 until piece measures same length as center panel. Repeat row 6 once, row 5 once, and rows 1–3. Bind off in pattern.

Left side panel: 25 stitches
Rows 1–4: K 1, p 1, repeat across to end.
Row 5: (K 1, p 1) 2 times, (k 4, p 1) 2 times, (k 1, p 1) repeat to end of row.

NANTUCKET CABLE. Knitted rug designed and made by Elizabeth Malament.

Row 6: (K 1, p 1) 5 times, k 1, (k 1, p 4) 2 times, k 1, p 1, k 1.

Row 7: (K 1, p 1) 2 times, cable on next 4 stitches, p 1, k 4, p 1, (k 1, p 1) to end.

Row 8: Repeat row 6.

Row 9: Repeat row 5.

Row 10: Repeat row 6.

Row 11: (K 1, p 1) 2 times, k 4, p 1, cable on next 4 sts, (p 1, k 1) to end.

Row 12: Repeat row 6.

Row 13: Repeat row 5.

Row 14: Repeat row 6.

Row 15: Repeat row 7.

Repeat rows 8–15 until piece measures same length as other panels.
Repeat row 6 once, row 5 once, and rows 1–3. Bind off in pattern.

Sew together neatly and fringe. (See chapter on finishing.)

PARIS STRIPE. Knitted rug designed and made by Elizabeth Malament.

Materials:

      Rug yarn: 4 skeins main color (MC)

              2½ skeins color A

      1 pair knitting needles, size 11

Note:

      All color changes must be done on the same side of the work.

Stitch:

      The entire rug is worked in garter stitch, knit all rows.

With MC cast on one stitch. Increase one stitch (st), at the end of each row until there are 45 sts. Drop MC and attach color A.

With color A, continue in the same way until there are 79 sts. Drop color A and attach MC.

Working in the same way, with one st more each row, knit 6 rows MC (85 sts), 10 rows color A (95 sts), 5 rows MC (100 sts).

Next row, with MC omit increases (100 sts). Drop MC, attach color A. The end of this row is the corner. In the next and every row thereafter, decrease one st at this corner end and continue to increase 1 st at the other end. Each row will have 100 sts. This section of 100 st rows consists of 10 rows of color A, 6 rows of MC, 28 rows of color A, 6 rows MC, 10 rows color A, 7 rows MC. This completes the next corner. At the end of the next row (MC) discontinue increases. At beginning of each row decrease 1 st until all sts have been decreased. The decreasing section is to be worked with MC 3 more rows, 10 rows in color A, 6 rows MC, 34 rows in color A, complete in MC to the end.

Fringe.

DUET. Shown with partial vertical rows of weaving.

DUET

Materials:

Rug yarn: 1 main color

1 or 2 colors for weaving

1 pair knitting needles, size 11

1 crochet hook or large needle for weaving

Cast on an uneven number of stitches.

Row 1: Knit.

Row 2: K 2, *yarn over needle, k 2 together, repeat from * ending with k 1.

Row 3: Knit.

Row 4: K 1, *yarn over needle, k 2 together, repeat from * ending with k 2 together.

Repeat rows 1–4 to desired length.

End with row 1 or 3.

Bind off in knitting.

Weaving may be done with vertical or diagonal rows of 3 strands of yarn over and under across rug, leaving 5 or 6 inches of yarn at each end for knotted fringe. Alternate over and under in each row.

DUET. Shown with diagonal rows of weaving.

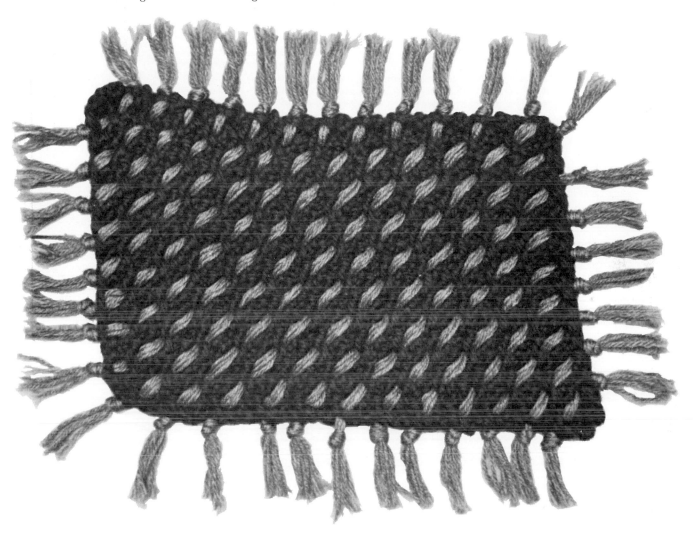

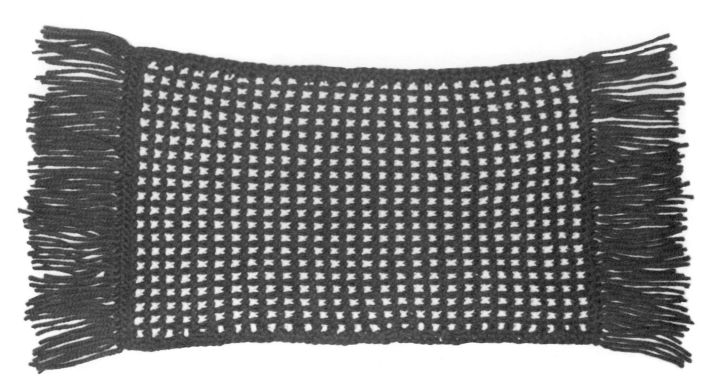

RHODE ISLAND REVERSIBLE. Knitted rug designed and made by Elizabeth Malament. Photographs show both sides of this reversible rug.

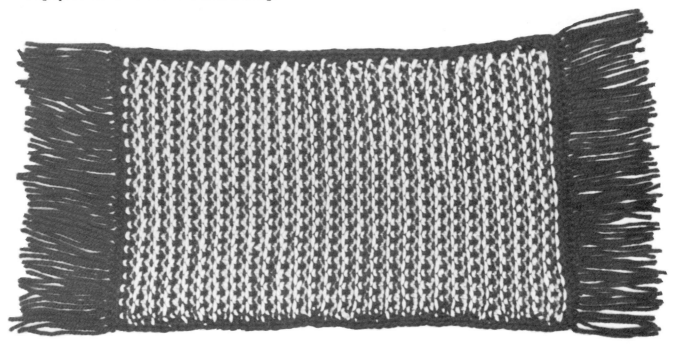

RHODE ISLAND REVERSIBLE

Materials:

Rug yarn: Light color A
Dark color B

1 pair knitting needles, size 11

Note:

A rug no wider than 15–16 inches can be worked in one piece. If a wider rug is desired, it should be worked in strips and sewn together neatly.

With color B, cast on an odd number of stitches (depending on size you require).

Row 1: With color B, knit.

Row 2: Repeat row 1.

Row 3: With color A, k 1, *keeping yarn in back, slip 1 purlwise, k 1, repeat from * ending with k 1.

Row 4: With color A, k 1, *keeping thread in front, slip 1 purlwise, k 1, repeat from * ending with k 1.

Repeat rows 1–4 for desired length.

Bind off in color B.

Finish with one row of single crochet around, 3 single crochet in each corner.

Fringe.

STEPHANIE. Knitted rug designed by Elizabeth Malament and made by Stephanie Goodstein. (See color plate 32)

Materials:

    Rug yarn: Color A, ⅙ of total quantity

             Color B, ⅖ of total quantity

             Color C, ⅗ of total quantity

    1 pair knitting needles, size 11

    1 double-pointed needle for cable

Note:

    The rug is made by winding one long knitted cable into an oval shape.

    The cable twists are done every 8 rows.

Stitch:

    The cable is done on 6 sts. On the cable row, p 1, slip 3 sts to double-pointed needle and hold in the back; k 3, k 3 from double-pointed needle, p 1.

Cast on 8 stitches in color.

Row 1: P 1, k 6, p 1.

Row 2: K 1, p 6, k 1.

Rows 3–8: Repeat row 1 and row 2.

Row 9: P 1, cable on next 6, p 1.

Repeat rows 2 through 9.

When you have enough of color A, switch to color B and continue knitting in same way. You will need more of color B than A as your oval is now larger.

When you have knitted enough to make three complete circles, change to color C.

You can make this rug any size, shape, and color combination you desire.

Sew together and press.

BORDERS. Woven rug designed and woven by Florence Friedman.

10 SIMPLE WOVEN RUGS

INTRODUCTION

The history of weaving dates back more than 20,000 years, when primitive man developed his own crude form of weaving, which consisted of braiding grass and twigs. Through the centuries spindles and looms were developed, and today, with modern equipment readily available, weaving is a popular creative hobby. The basic principles of weaving have remained the same, however, from primitive times to the present, in spite of all the new machinery.

As the loom and designs get more complex, weaving becomes more difficult. Actually, weaving is a broad field and requires a book to itself. I shall therefore only discuss the simplest form of weaving. If it intrigues you, I suggest that you learn more about weaving and, perhaps, take some lessons so that you can master this exciting skill.

THE MECHANICS OF WEAVING

Weaving consists of interlacing a set of vertical threads with a set of horizontal threads, forming a solid fabric. The vertical threads are called the *warp*. What you fill in, or the horizontal threads, are called the *weft*. (The device that I used as a youngster to distinguish the warp from the weft was to associate warp with harp, which also has vertical strings). The individual rows are called *picks*.

The warp has a fixed number of threads or "ends" that are stretched onto a loom (a frame) . To help with the interlacing, the yarn used for the weft is wound onto a shuttle. In order to do the over and under weaving, looms have a "shedding" motion that picks up the over and under threads separately. The *harnesses* make this shedding possible.

This woven rug appeared as part of the Russian People's Art at the Second Pan-Russian Exhibition of peasant industries in Petrograd in 1913. It was woven in 1796. The initials are those of the person for whom the rug was made.

The more complex the loom, the more harnesses it will have. The warp threads are threaded into the harnesses. Treadles, or levers, control the movement of each harness. When you depress a particular treadle or lever, all the warp ends that have been threaded through heddles (sets of vertical cords or wires) on that harness will go up, while the other warp ends remain below. The space between is called the *shed*. The shuttle will go through this shed in one motion.

In plain weaving, all the even warp ends are in one harness; all the odd warp ends in another. As you do each row, it is "beaten" or pushed down. On most looms, a built-in beater, stretching all the way across the loom, has a comblike reed that does the beating. This reed is changeable, allowing for fine or coarse work.

For the purpose of the beginner, I will describe a technique of weaving on a simple frame loom. With this method, you can make woven or rya squares that can be sewn together to make any size rug.

EQUIPMENT

The Frame Loom

A simple frame loom can be made from a wooden stretcher used by artists, or from strips of wood you put together yourself. Try to use hardwood, which won't split readily, and clamp or bolt the corners together. The size should be one that is comfortable for you to handle.

Place 3-inch finishing nails along the top and bottom of the frame 1 inch from the edge, ½ inch apart. These nails will hold the warp. If the nails do not go in easily, try drilling holes for each nail.

Loom. Rising shed (jack loom).

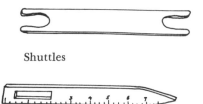

Shuttles

Shuttle

You will need a shuttle to carry the weft across the warp. Make a shuttle from a flat piece of wood with cutouts at each end, over which you wind the weft. Or just use a 12-inch ruler with a hole drilled at one end to hold the weft.

Warp Threads

The warp threads should be very strong and elastic so that they will spring back after being stretched to make a shed. Warp threads take a great deal of abuse during the filling process, so try to obtain a strong spun linen. If spun linen is not available, a heavy crochet cotton can be used.

To make the warp, start in the upper left-hand corner and tie a slip knot onto the first nail. Now go down to the lower left-hand corner and go around the nails marked 2 and 3. Next go up and around 4 and 5. Continue in this way all across the loom, making certain that the warp is kept tight and the tension even at all times. Tie the thread to the last nail.

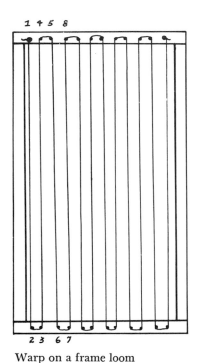

Warp on a frame loom

Shed Sticks

Shed sticks are used to open a shed to allow the shuttle to go right through. You will need two plain, flat, thin sticks (a yardstick will do) that are cut slightly longer than the width of the frame and which you will weave through the warp. Make sure the edges are not rough. Sandpaper them if necessary.

Weave each shed stick into the warp in a flat position, the first over and under, the second under and over (in opposite order). When these sticks are turned in an upright position, they will make the shed for the shuttle carrying the weft thread.

Weft

The weft does not have to be strong, as it does not bear the brunt of the weaving process. Yarns of different fibers and weights can be used. Whatever you decide to use must be wound around the shuttle. Do not wind too much yarn at one time or it will be difficult to go through the shed.

WEAVING PROCEDURES

Start to weave at the lower right-hand corner. In order to provide a firm base, which in turn will keep your first row of weaving straight, start to weave with cloth strips (old torn sheets will serve this purpose), which you will later pull out. It is very important to have your first row of weft straight or all the following rows will be crooked. Turn the first shed stick on its side to open a shed and pass the shuttle with the cloth strip through the shed. Leave a tail on the side so you can pull it out when you have finished all the weaving. Now open the other shed by lowering the first shed stick and raising the second. Now pass a cloth strip through. Weave with cloth for about 1 inch before you start with your regular weft. If you are planning to have a fringed edge, weave with cloth for about 4 inches. When you pull out these strips, you will use the exposed warp ends for knotting and fringes. When you start to weave with your proper filling, pass the shuttle through the shed to the left, leaving a 2-inch tail at the right edge. Insert this tail into the second shed or darn it into the woven material after work is completed. As you weave, you will have to beat the weft down tightly. Use a heavy comb or kitchen fork to push the weft threads as close together as possible. Try to have an even number of picks per inch. Measure frequently to check. If there is a variation, you may be inconsistent in your beating (combing).

Make sure that your first row of weft is straight so that the following rows will also be straight. As you go across each row, the weft is put through on a diagonal, starting down and going up to allow for the extra length used up in the interlacing process. The selvages have a tendency to pull in and narrow as you work. To avoid this, measure width frequently.

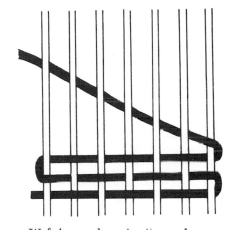

Weft inserted on the diagonal

Selvages

It is important to keep the selvages neat and straight. Each time you go around the edge to start a new row, place the weft thread carefully into position around the first warp end so that it doesn't pull in too tightly. It should be so loose that a loop is formed at the edge.

Starting a New Thread

If you are starting a new piece of thread of the same color, just lay the new thread beside the old one in the same shed, overlapping them for about 2 inches.

When you are weaving with more than one color and they are not far apart in the design, you can carry the thread along the side of the loom as illustrated rather than cutting and starting a new end.

The first end of a new color is treated the same way as the first pick.

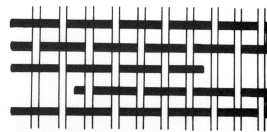

Starting a new thread

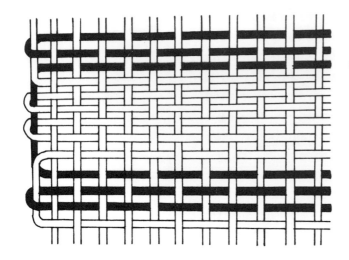

Carrying thread along the side

Removing from Frame

Cut through top of first and second warp threads and tie together. Cut bottom of first and second warp threads and tie together. Continue cutting and tying pairs until all weft threads are cut and tied.

RYA WEAVING PROCEDURES

Rya weaving is a combination of plain weaving and Turkish or Ghiordes knots. There is a great deal of flexibility with design and color in this technique. There are two ways to prepare the yarn for the knots —you can either cut it to size or work from a "butterfly;" which is described below in greater detail.

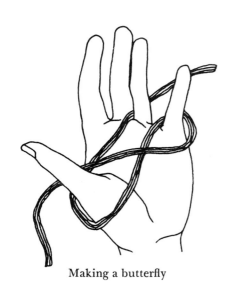

Making a butterfly

The butterfly

Cutting Yarn

Decide how long you want your pile to be. Remember that the knot will take about ½ inch, so if you want a 2-inch pile, cut pieces 4½ inches long. A 1½-inch pile take a 3½-inch piece. See directions in the chapter on latch hooking for cutting yarn, pages 94–95.

Keep colors separated as you cut. A cardboard box with compartments is handy to keep near your loom.

Working with a Butterfly

Instead of cutting individual pieces for each knot, you can work with continuous strands and cut the loops after each row.

Combine three or four strands of any color or colors you select. Wind these together and hold in a butterfly. Do not make it so thick that it won't pass through the shed easily. Pass the butterfly through the warp, keeping pile a consistent length. You can use a gauge or just trust your eye. Ryas with uneven pile have an interesting look.

Set up (dress) the loom as you would for regular weaving.

Weaving

The number of picks of plain weaving between each row of knots depends on how dense you want the pile to be. The more rows between knotted rows, the shaggier your rya will be. If you use a 2-inch pile, 1 inch of woven weft is about average.

To make strong vertical edges, yarn is tied to both sides of the warp to be wrapped around the edges as you go along. Or you can leave a pair of warp threads at each side unknotted.

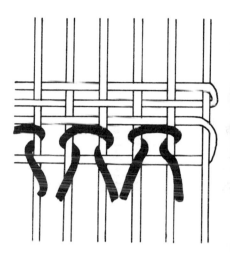

Wrapping warp edges

The Ghiordes Knot

This knot uses two warp threads per knot. Work the knot when the shed is closed. Starting from the left, place a piece of the cut pile over two warp threads. If yarn is lightweight, combine two, three, or even four strands for each knot. Subtle colors combined in one knot are frequently used for exciting effects. Wrap the ends around the two warp threads as in illustration at right. Pull tightly against last row of pick. The next pick will hold the knot in place.

Ghiordes knot

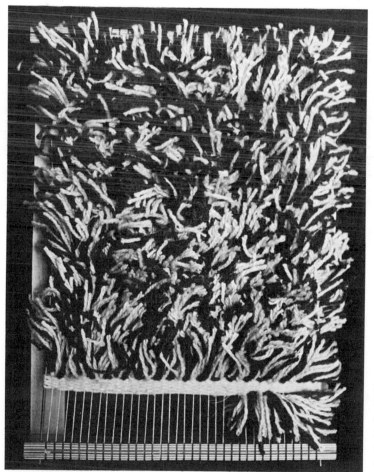

Rya square on simple frame loom. Notice rows of simple weaving between rows of rya knots. These rows do not show up in the completed rug.

181

Variations

For interesting variations you can make the length of the pile uneven. The rya at the top of page 184 used as a wall hanging adds interest by introducing beads, which are strung onto the pile before it is knotted.

The second rya on page 184 has some pile as long as 7 inches held down by a horizontal bar of yarn stitched over it.

Rya lends itself to experimentation. It is easy to remove a knot, so don't be afraid to try an idea—as wild as it may seem to you.

Design ideas for rya and woven rugs. Designed by Daga Ramsey.

Yugoslavian rya and woven wall hanging. Designed and made by Marijan. Collection of Port Washington Art Gallery.

FORMS. Designed and made by Florence Friedman. A square, a triangle, and a circle were used to design this rya done on a loom with simple weaving between rows of knots.

JACK'S RUG. Woven rug designed and made by Florence Friedman. Design is suitable for hooked, latched, or embroidered rugs. (See color plate 33)

186

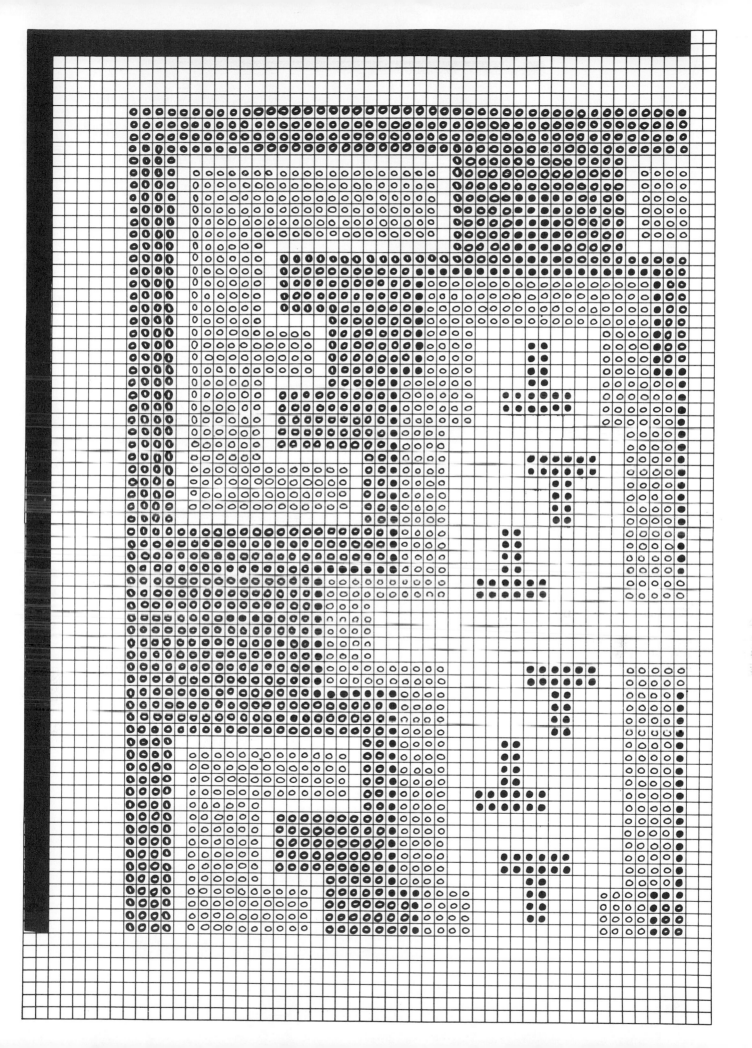

DOUBLE ARROW. Woven rug
designed and made by
Florence Friedman.
(See color plate 34)

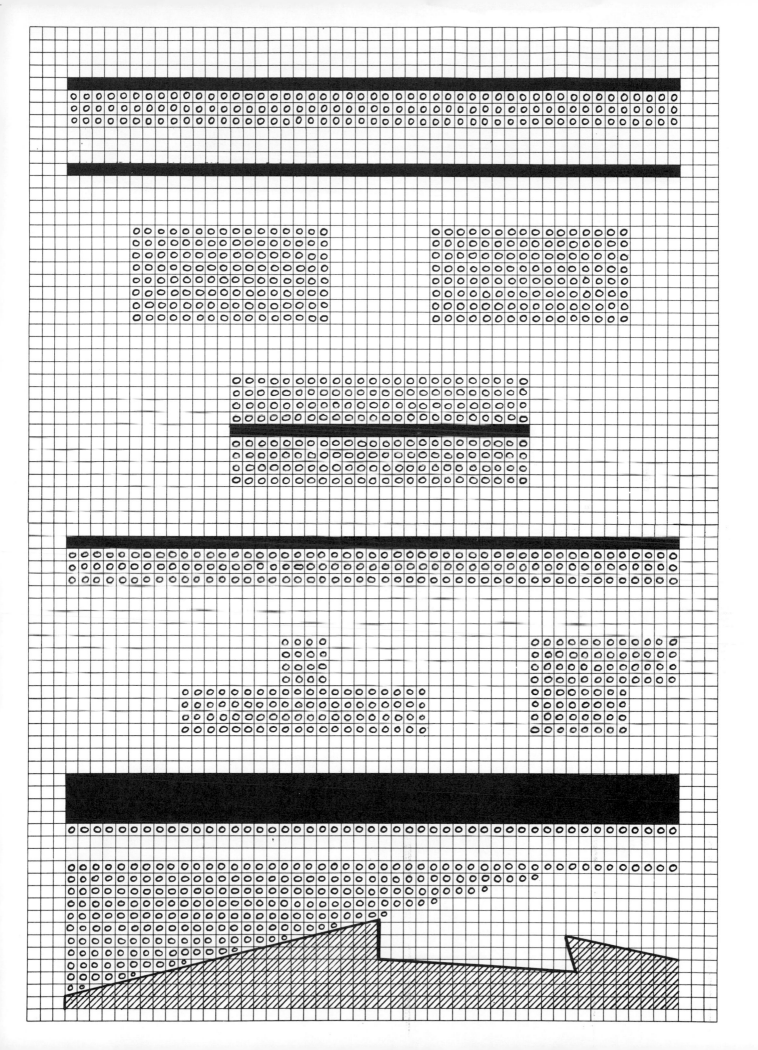

ANIMAL CRACKERS. Woven Polish wall hanging. Author's collection. Design
suitable for hooked, latch hooked, and embroidered rugs. (See color plate 35)

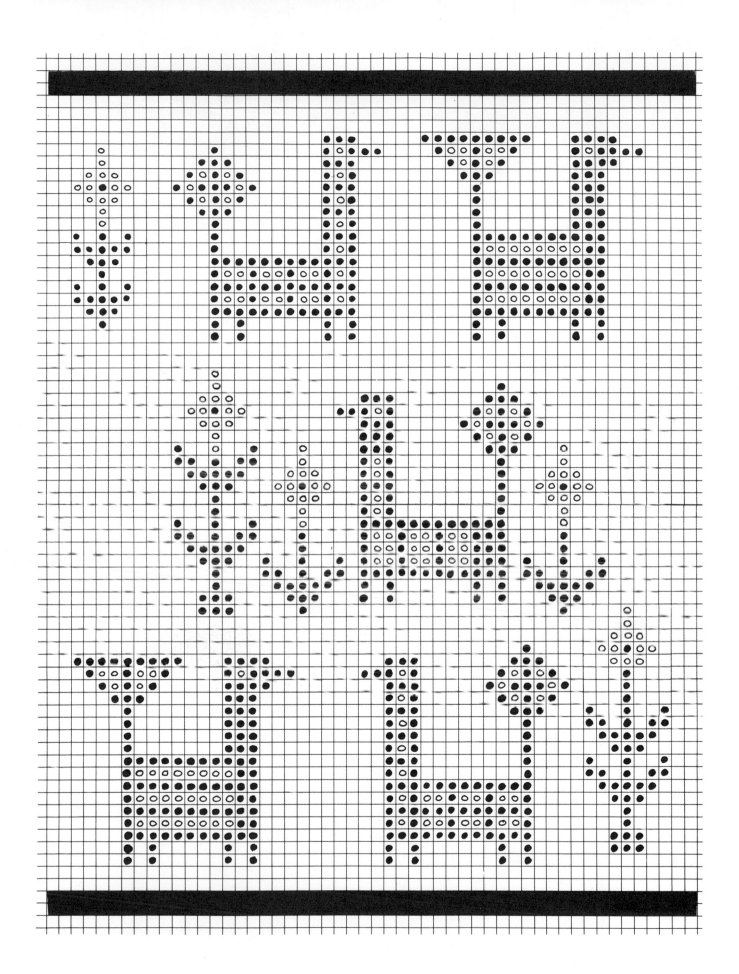

Nineteenth-century Ukranian woven rug.

Nineteenth-century Ukranian woven rug.

11 DYEING

INTRODUCTION

Dyeing is really a simple process and one you will find useful once you became addicted to rug making. Bits of odd-colored fabrics can be dyed to make one color family. Remember that it is easier to dye light colors darker than it is to dye dark colors lighter. Tone down harsh colors by giving them a grey wash. Streaking or uneven coloring won't hurt your finished rug. In fact, it may make it more interesting.

In the old days, before one could go to a store to buy almost anything one needed, dyes were made from natural things gathered in the woods or from the kitchen garden. Today, commercial dyes are available in a multitude of colors. By following the simple directions on the package, you will be able to get just the shade you want. Experiment by mixing various colors together and using strong and weak solutions. If you are using new yarns, get natural, undyed yarns. Wool flannel is available undyed also. Naturally, if you are using older fabrics you will have to dye whatever is available and experiment. The original color will affect the final color. Black is impossible to dye over.

Strippers are available which will remove color. This, of course, will add an extra step to the process but might prove necessary when you are short of light colors.

Prepare used fabric as described in the chapter on Braided Rugs, page 62. This process will make dyeing simple. Wet wool will be more receptive to the dye than dry wool.

MORDANTS

If you are a brave soul and would like to try the dyeing methods of our ancestors, I have listed at the end of this chapter some of the main natural color sources. Many natural dyes will fade or "bleed" unless the yarn or fabric is first treated with a chemical called a mordant. The word *mordant* comes from the Latin *mordere,* meaning "to bite" and refers to any substance that is applied for the purpose of fixing the color.

Some common mordants used with natural dyes are:

Alum (potassium aluminum sulfate): Use 2 to 4 ounces of alum for each pound of wool.

Chrome (bichromate of potash): Use ¼ ounce to ½ ounce of chrome for each pound of wool. The use of chrome mordant produces very deep color.

Iron Sulfate (green vitriol): Use ¼ ounce for each pound of wool. One ounce of cream of tartar is also added to the solution to make the fabric colorfast.

Tin Crystals (stannous chloride): Use ½ ounce tin crystals and 1 ounce cream of tartar for each pound of wool.

Acetic Acid (white vinegar): A 40 percent solution of acetic acid, using 1 teaspoon to 1 gallon of warm water added to the dye bath, will help the wool to take up the dye.

Salt (not iodized): Use a tablespoon in a quart of warm water.

NATURAL DYEING PROCEDURES

Prepare the dye solution by chopping, then soaking and boiling the plant parts, and straining them out before adding their color to the dye bath. Be sure that the wool (or fabric) is clean and moist before placing it in the dye bath. For each pound of wool, use 4 to 4½ gallons of dye bath; add wool when the dye bath is lukewarm. Heat slowly to simmering point and let simmer for ½ hour (longer if a darker color is desired), moving wool gently back and forth. Rinse dyed wool, squeeze out moisture, and dry in the shade.

Equipment

    A large enamel or stainless steel pot
    A long-handled wooden fork for stirring
    A pan for rinsing
    Rubber gloves

Procedure

Have enough water in the large pot to cover yarn or fabric to be dyed. Add the dye color to the water and stir thoroughly. Put wet material into dye pot which is barely simmering. If you want an even color, do not crowd in the pot. Stir constantly until the color has left the water and has been absorbed by the wool. Remove from the dye pot. Add mordant to water and return yarn or fabric to the pot. Stir once or twice, then remove wool. A wooden drying rack in your bath tub is a good place to hang the dripping material. When most of the dripping has stopped, rinse in warm water, then gradually in cooler water. If you use cold water, the fabric might stiffen.

Keep accurate notes on your dyeing process in case you want to repeat a color. Keep a small sample of the dyed wool with the notes.

It is best to dye in daylight so that you can see exactly what colors you are getting. If this is not possible, use a daylight-type florescent light. Remember that colors seem darker when fabric is wet.

For background colors mottling will add interest. To get a mottled effect, crowd fabric into the pan so that it will not dye evenly. Keep just under the boiling point.

If your finished rug colors look too bright or harsh, expose the rug to the sun until the colors get a nice soft, dull look. If only one or two colors are too harsh, cover the rest of the rug with wrapping paper and cut holes to expose only the area you want dulled.

Dyeing with Skins of the Common Cooking Onion

The papery brown skins of the common cooking onion may be used to produce soft shades of yellow, gold, and burnt orange. No mordant is necessary, but deeper shades result when alum is used to mordant the wool. Boil 1 pound of skins for ½ hour. Strain the liquid into bath for the dye. Steep wet wool for ½ hour to 1 hour in the hot dye bath. Rinse and dry.

Natural Dyeing Color Sources

DYESTUFF	SOURCE	COLOR	MORDANT	NOTES
Alder	Bark, leaves	Black	Iron sulfate	
	Bark	Brown	Iron sulfate	
Azalea	Leaves	Dark gray	Weak iron sulfate	
	Leaves	Brownish red	Slaked lime	Pick leaves in fall
Bayberry	Leaves	Grayish green	Alum	Pick leaves in summer
Blackberry	Young shoots	Light gray-black	Alum	Add iron sulfate to darken color
Black walnut	Green outer husks	Dark brown-black	No mordant needed but soak husks for twenty-four hours	Pick husks while green. Remove with hammer.
Blueberry	Berry	Blue-purple	Alum	
Dandelion	Roots	Purple	No mordant needed	
	Whole plant	Magenta	No mordant needed	
Elderberry	Berry	Blue	Salt	Crush berries before soaking. Depth of color depends on amount used and length of boiling time.
	Berry	Lilac	Alum	
	Berry	Violet purple	Chrome	
	Leaves	Green	Alum	
Goldenrod	Flower	Yellow-tan	Alum	Pick when flowers are just about to bloom
		Old gold	Chrome	
Lily of the valley	Leaves	Lime	Chrome	Pick in spring
		Greenish gold	Chrome	Pick in fall
Marigold	Flower	Yellow to gold	Alum	Add a few walnut husks for a deeper tone
Maple	Bark	Gray to purple	Iron sulfate	
	Bark	Olive	Alum	
Nettle	Whole plant	Greenish-yellow	Alum	Wear gloves when picking
Onion	Dried skins from common cooking onion	Golden yellow	Alum	Mordant wool first with alum
		Burnt orange	Alum with tin	
		Brass yellow	Crome	
		Olive green	Alum with iron sulfate	
Pomegranate	Hard outer skin	Yellow	Alum	
		Brown	Very weak solution iron sulfate	
		Violet blue	Above solution plus ash extract	
Privet	Berries	Blue, brue-green	Alum and salt	Add yarn when crushed berries are boiling
	Berries and leaves	Green	Alum	
	Leaves and	Yellow	Alum and cream of tartar	
	branch tips	Gold	Chrome	

Natural Dyeing Color Sources

DYESTUFF	SOURCE	COLOR	MORDANT	NOTES
Saffron	Flowers or powder from grocery	Yellow	Alum	
Sumac	Berries	Yellowish tan to gray	Alum and iron sulfate	Pick when fully ripe. Crush fruit before overnight soaking. Add iron sulfate after dye.
	Leaves, twig	Brown to tan	None	
White birch	Leaves	Yellow	Alum	Longer boiling will produce a deeper yellow
	Leaves and twig	Yellowish green	Alum	
	Inner bark	Brown	None	Break bark into small bits before soaking

12 FINISHING

Finishing is important if your rug is to look neat and wear well. If you want to spend the money, professional finishing is always worthwhile. When you think that most handmade rugs will outlive you and probably your heirs, the cost becomes minimal. Finishing your work yourself, however, does add to the pride of a job well done, so if you want to make a rug from start to finish, the instructions below will help you.

BLOCKING

Rugs—especially embroidered rugs—will require blocking if they have lost their shape during the working process. Blocking is not always an easy job, as the canvas may be terribly distorted. These days most upholsterers and art shops are experienced at handling embroidered canvas and will do justice to your work.

If you should decide to do the finishing yourself, you will need a few pieces of equipment: a large board, plywood, or a drawing board that is several inches larger than your rug; a draftsman's T square; a large plastic triangle with a 90-degree corner; rustproof pushpins (I prefer pushpins to thumbtacks, as they are easier to remove), a large towel, and a sponge.

Place the towel on the board, and put the canvas face down on the towel. With a wet sponge thoroughly moisten the canvas. Do not be afraid to use water; if you have used colorfast ink or paint on your canvas, nothing will run. Pin the top edge of the work parallel to the top edge of the board. Pull the bottom into shape, making sure that the corners form right angles. Check by using the T square or a large plastic triangle, and make sure that your canvas is evenly taut. Pin all around the canvas at approximately one-inch intervals. Allow two or three days for complete drying. Keep the board in a horizontal position and avoid artificial heat during the drying process.

When you remove the canvas from the board, you might want to steam it briefly to restore the natural fluff. Hold the steam iron over the right side, making sure that you do not touch the yarn with the iron. The steam will do the work.

If you have worked your rug in sections to be joined later, block each of your sections separately.

JOINING

If you have made your hooked, embroidered, latched, or rya in sections, you will want to join them. Make two lines of machine stitches about ½ inch apart around the four sides of the backing margin of each piece. Trim as close to the stitching as possible. Overlap backing and baste together with strong thread. Work across the joining with appropriate color and method, going through the two thicknesses. The seam will hardly be distinguishable. Try to plan your design so that the joining stitches are part of the pattern.

Crocheted and knitted rugs use the same yarn for finishing as was used for the rug. Place sections face down in the proper positions. Start joining by looping yarn through a stitch to secure it, then lace from side to side on the outside stitches, being careful to align sections neatly.

BINDING

Edges

There are various methods for finishing the edges.

You can fold and baste the foundation fabric toward the top 1 inch all around before you start to work a pile rug. You will then work through a double thickness, and the raw edges will be hidden by the pile. I do not like this method because I find it too difficult to work through the double thickness and it cannot be used on oval or round rugs. Some people prefer it to other methods because when the stitching is finished the rug is finished.

Another method is to stitch a cotton rug tape the color of the outer edge of your work to the right side of the backing fabric before you begin to work. (I dye tape if I can't get the right color.) When you are ready to work along the edges, thumbtack the binding to the frame to keep it out of the way. When you have finished all the stitches, cut backing fabric ¾ inch from the edge. Next, turn the tape to the wrong side and hemstitch.

The method I prefer is done after all the stitching is completed. Sew cotton rug tape to the right side of the rug as close to the worked edge as possible, using strong thread and a small running or backstitch. To keep edge really firm, I sometimes sew a second row of stitching about ⅛ inch from the first row. Then trim backing to about ¾ inch all around. Next, turn the binding to the back and hem all around. Don't pull tape too tightly, rather ease the tape to the rug. For oval or round rugs you should use a bias tape. If you can't find one, make your own from a strong cotton fabric cut about 2 inches wide. Don't ease bias tape to oval or round rugs; it is better in this case to stretch it slightly.

On soft foundations such as monk's cloth, binding is not really necessary. Simply turn hem allowances to the back, making sure that you fold it as close to the last row of work as possible. Baste along this edge. Turn in a ½-inch hem at raw edge and baste. Hemstitch to rug.

Corners

In order to avoid bulky corners, cut a piece from the backing before you miter the corners. Then fold one side down and overcast, then fold and overcast the other side, and then the diagonal. When you hemstitch the binding, miter each corner as you come to it.

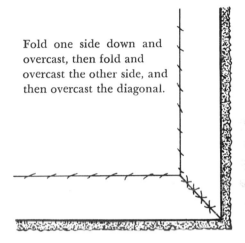

Cut a piece from the backing before you miter the corners.

Fold one side down and overcast, then fold and overcast the other side, and then overcast the diagonal.

FRINGE

Some rugs may look incomplete without a fringe. Use your own judgment about fringe, and if you do decide to put one on, consider the length, color, and texture carefully. Try a few pieces of fringe of varying lengths and thicknesses before you cut all the pieces. You can use the yarn from the rug, or butcher's cord of a neutral off-white color. Woven rugs will have their own fringe from the warp threads.

Make certain that you leave room on the rug ends for pulling the fringe through. If you hem the rug first, pull fringe through the double thickness. Crocheted and knitted rugs should have fringe attached between the first and second row of stitches. The space between each fringe depends on the number of strands you use for each group. The more strands, the further apart each one will be. When you decide on a length, cut each strand double that length, plus 1 inch for knotting. If you want to braid the fringe, allow more length. Practice first, then measure the length needed. Attach the fringe with a crochet hook. Fold each group of strands in half and pull through edge. Slip

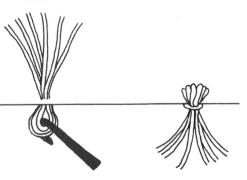

To make fringes, fold each group of strands in half and pull through edge with crochet hook. Slip ends through the loop and pull tightly to secure the knot.

ends through the loop and pull tightly to secure the knot. Space evenly along edges. For an unusual effect, you can braid the fringe as shown on page 118.

For braided rugs you can use a self fringe as shown in design on page 70.

LINING

If your rug is bound firmly, there is no need to line it. I think lining tends to hold in dirt and gravel, and eventually this will weaken your pile. If you do want a lining, use a tightly woven cotton or linen. Turn binding and sew a small running stitch about $\frac{3}{16}$ inch down from edge. This will keep binding in place. Now pin or baste lining under the binding and hemstitch binding to lining.

Unlined rugs can be protected by applying a rubberized or latex backing. This liquid latex is applied with a paintbrush. It will protect hooked rugs from pulling out and will keep your rug from sliding. Many people object to the stiffness of the latex backing and prefer to use thick padding under their rugs.

CARE

Pressing

When your rug is bound, you might want to press it into shape. Put it face down on paper on the floor. Wet a large piece of toweling, wring it out, and place it over the rug. Press over the towel with a hot iron. Don't move the rug until it is thoroughly dry.

Cleaning

If your rug gets dusty, don't shake it or hang it on a line. This will weaken the rug. Use a vacuum that does not have a beating action, and vacuum both sides. Occasionally turn your rugs upside down for a few days. This will loosen imbedded dirt.

If you have soil spots, you can hand-wash the rug in cold water and detergent. Make certain that colors don't run; if you have followed my instructions, they shouldn't. Never put your handmade rug in a washing machine.

Storing

If you want to store your rugs, never fold them, as this puts a strain on the backing. The best method is to roll the rug right-side out over some paper rolls.

BIBLIOGRAPHY

Aller, Doris. *Handmade Rugs.* Menlo Park, Calif.: Lane Publishing Company, 1959.

Amsden, Charles Avery. *Navaho Weaving, Its Technique and History.* Santa Ana, Calif.: The Fine Arts Press, 1934.

Bowles, Ella S. *Handmade Rugs.* Garden City: Garden City Publishing Company, 1937.

Brinley, Rosemary. *Rug-Making.* Marjorie O'Shaughnessy (ed.). New York: Dover Publications, 1952.

Butler, Winifred. *Needlework and Embroidery.* London: Pan Books, Ltd., 1966.

Caulfield, S. F. A. *Encyclopedia of Victorian Needlework.* 2 vols. New York: Dover Publications, 1972.

Droop, Joan. *Rug Making.* Newton Centre, Mass.: Charles Branford Company, 1971.

Duncan, Ida. *The Complete Book of Needlecraft.* New York: Liveright Publishing Company, 1961.

Feeley, Helen Howard. *The Complete Book of Rug Braiding.* New York: Coward-McCann, Inc., 1963.

Formenton, Fabio. *Oriental Rugs and Carpets.* New York: McGraw Hill, 1972.

Harbeson, Georgiana Brown. *American Needlework.* New York: Bonanza Books, 1938.

Hedin, Salweig, and Springer, Jo. *Creative Needlework.* New York: Arco Publishing Company, 1969.

Kahlenberg, Mary Hunt, and Berlant, Anthony. *The Navajo Blanket.* New York: Praeger Publishers, 1972.

Laury, Jean Ray, and Aiken, Joyce. *Handmade Rugs.* Philadelphia: Countryside Press, Farm Journal, Inc., 1972.

Lichten, Frances. *Folk Art of Rural Pennsylvania.* New York: Bonanza Books, 1956.

Liebetrau, Preben. *Oriental Rugs in Color.* New York: The Macmillan Company, 1969.

Marinoff, Kathryn. *Getting Started in Handmade Rugs*. New York: Bruce Publishing Company, 1971.

Mathews, Sibyl. *Needle Made Rugs*. London: Mills Boon, Ltd., 1960.

Maxwell, Gilbert. *Navajo Rugs, Past, Present, and Future*. Palm Desert, Calif.: Best-West Publications, 1963.

McGown, Pearl K. *You Can Hook Rugs*. Sturbridge, Mass.: Lincoln House, 1951.

Parker, Xenia Ley. *Hooked Rugs and Ryas*. Chicago: Henry Regnery Company, 1973.

Rex, Stella Hay. *Choice Hooked Rugs*. Englewood Cliffs, N.J.: Prentice-Hall, Inc., 1953.

Stewart, Janice S. *The Folk Arts of Norway*. Madison, Wisconsin: University of Wisconsin Press, 1953.

Tattersoll, C. E. C. *Notes on Carpet-Knotting and Weaving*. London: Her Majesty's Stationery Office, 1969.

Van Cura, Joan. *Braiding Rugs the Easy Way*. Southold, N.Y.: Van Cura, 1964.

Wilcox, Bettina. *Hooked Rugs for Fun and Profit*. New York: Homecrafts, 1949.

Willcox, Donald J. *Techniques of Rya Knotting*. New York: Van Nostrand Reinhold Company, 1971.

Williams, Elsa S. *Creative Canvas Work*. New York: Van Nostrand Reinhold Company, 1972.

Zarback, Barbara J. *The Complete Book of Rug Hooking*. New York: Van Nostrand Reinhold Company, 1961.

Znamierowski, Neil. *Step-by-Step Rugmaking*. Racine, Wisconsin: Western Publishing Company, 1972.

INDEX

Adjustable punch hook, 20
  how to use, 30–32
  proper position for holding, 32
  threading, 31
Alder (dyestuff), 197
Alum (mordant), 195
Azalea (dyestuff), 197

Backing, rubberized or latex, 202
Backing canvas, for latch hooked rugs,
  93–94
Backing foundation, for rya rug, 80
Basketweave stitch, 110
  embroidered rug designs for, 118–119,
    122–125, 128–131, 134–135, 136–137,
    138, 139
Bayberry (dyestuff), 197
Bent-handled scissors, 25
Bind off, 163
Binding, 200–201
Black walnut (dyestuff), 197
Blackberry (dyestuff), 197
Blocking, 199–200
Blueberry (dyestuff), 197
Borders, hooked rug, 27
Braided rugs, 60–75
  designs, 70–75
    chair pad, antique, 75
    cloverleaf rug, 71, 73
    oval, antique, 75
    panel rug, 70, 72
    rectangle, 70
    rectangle done in strips, 70
    rectangle formed from four or five
      ovals, 70, 71, 72
    round rugs with rows of braiding, 73
    runner, 74
    wheel rug, 70–71, 72

equipment, 61
fabric, 62
finishing, 69
history of, 61
preparation, 62–64
  color, 64
  cutting the strips, 62–63
  folding strips, 63
  rolling strips into coils or wheels, 63–
    64
  sewing strips, 63
procedures, 65–69
  braiding, 65
  changing colors, 67
  increasing, 69
  lacing, 68–69
  modified square turns, 66
  oval rug, 66, 67
  round rug, 66, 67
  square knot, 69
  square rug, 67
  starting to braid, 65
shape of, 61
tapering, 69
Burlap, 21
Butterfly, making a, 180

Canvas, types of (for embroidered rugs),
  107–108
Care of rugs, 202
Casting on, 162
Chain stitch, 142
China (ancient), 13
Chrome (mordant), 195
Cleaning the rug, 202
Cloverleaf rug (combination of braiding
  and hooking), 71

Common cooking onion, dyeing with skins
  of, 196
Continental stitch, 109
  embroidered rug designs for, 114–115,
    116–117, 118–119, 120–121, 122–125,
    128–131, 134–135, 136–137, 139
Corners, binding, 201
Crochet hook, 141–142
  attaching fringe with, 201–202
Crocheted rugs, 140–159
  designs, 144–159
    doily (or hexagon) shape, 154–155
    with fringe, 150–151, 152–153
    oval, 144–145
    single crochet used as background for
      pile, 159
    spoked and solid squares, 158
    square, 146–147, 156–157, 158
    square with circle in it, 156–157
    using jute thread, 148–149
  equipment, 141–142
    crochet hooks, 141–142
    types of threads to use, 142
  fringe, 201–202
  history of, 141
  stitches, 142–144
    chain stitch, 142
    decrease, 144
    double crochet, 142, 143
    how to begin, 142
    increase, 144
    single crochet, 142, 143
    slip stitch, 144
    yarn over, 142, 143
Cross-stitch, 111, 113
  embroidered rug designs for, 134–135
Cutting machine (for strips of fabric), 22

Dandelion (dyestuff), 197
Decrease (in crochet stitch), 144
Decrease (in knitting), 162–163
Designs
    braided rugs, 70–75
        chair pad, antique, 75
        cloverleaf rug, 71, 73
        oval, antique, 75
        panel rug, 70, 72
        rectangle, 70
        rectangle done in strips, 70
        rectangle formed from four or five
            ovals, 70, 71, 72
        round rugs with rows of braiding, 73
        runner, 74
        wheel rug, 70–71, 72
    crocheted rugs, 144–159
        doily (or hexagon) shape, 154–155
        with fringe, 150–151, 152–153
        oval, 144–145
        single crochet used as background for
            pile, 159
        spoked and solid squares, 158
        square, 146–147, 156–157, 158
        square with circle in it, 156–157
        using jute thread, 148–149
    embroidered rugs, 113–139
        antique, 126–127
        Navajo motif, 114, 132–133
        needlepoint, 114–125, 128–131, 134–139
        using basketweave stitch, 109, 118–
            119, 122–125, 128–131, 134–135,
            136–137, 138, 139
        using continental stitch, 114–115, 116–
            117, 118–119, 120–121, 122–125, 128–
            131, 134–135, 136–137, 139
        using cross-stitches, 134–135
        using leftover yarn, 138
        using soumak (knitting) stitch, 126–
            127
    hooked rugs, 25–28, 34–60
        antique, 19, 38, 40–47, 50–51, 54–57,
            60
        borders, 27
        braided round (antique), 60
        creating your own, 25–27
        geometrics, 26, 49–50
        hit-or-miss, 26–27, 38, 39
        keeping it simple, 27
        leftover fabric (using up odds and
            ends), 38, 39
        rag rug, 19
        rags (through burlap), and left uncut
            for background, 16
        stair runner, 27, 59
        stair runner with matching rug, 36–37
        transferring onto foundation fabric,
            28
    knitted rugs, 163–173
        with diagonal rows, 169
        reversible rug, 170–171
        with vertical rows, 168
    latch hooked rugs, 97–105
        antique, 102, 103
        for child's room, 104, 105
        to enlarge, 99
        rya effect, 97
        tongue-shaped pattern, 97, 98
    pen wiper rugs, 76, 77
    rya rugs, 83–91
        wall hanging, 90, 91

simple woven rugs, 183–193
    nineteenth-century (Ukranian), 192,
        193
    peasant (Russian), 176
    square, triangle, and circle, 185
    wall hanging, 184, 190–191
Double crochet stitch, 142, 143
Dyeing, 194–198
    dyestuffs, 194–197
    introduction to, 194
    mordants for, 194–195
    natural procedures, 195–196
        for background colors, 196
        color sources (chart), 197–198
        with common onion skins, 196
        equipment, 195
        and exposing to the sun, 196
        how to begin, 195–196

Edges, binding, 200–201
Eggbeater hooks, how to use, 33
Egypt (ancient), 13
Elderberry (dyestuff), 197
Embroidered rugs, 106–139
    blocking, 199–200
    designs, 113–139
        antique, 126–127
        Navajo motif, 114, 132–133
        needlepoint, 114–125, 128–131, 134–
            139
        using basketweave stitch, 109, 118–
            119, 122–125, 128–131, 134–135, 136–
            137, 138, 139
        using continental stitch, 114–115, 116–
            117, 118–119, 120–121, 122–125, 128–
            131, 134–135, 136–137, 139
        using cross-stitches, 134–135
        using leftover yarn, 138
        using soumak (knitting) stitch, 126–
            127
    equipment, 107–109
        canvas, 107–108
        masking tape, 109
        needles, 108
        scissors, 108
        yarn, 108
    introduction to, 107
    stitches, 109–113
        basketweave, 110
        compensating for extra width and
            height, 113
        continental, 109
        cross-stitch, 111, 113
        long-legged cross-stitch, 111, 113
        rice stitch, 111, 113
        soumak (knitting) stitch, 111–112, 113
Encyclopedia of Victorian Needlework,
    The, 141, 161
Equipment
    for braided rugs, 61
    for crocheted rugs, 141–142
        crochet hooks, 141–142
        types of threads to use, 142
    for embroidered rugs, 107–109
        canvas, 107–108
        masking tape, 109
        needles, 108
        scissors, 108
        yarn, 108
    for hooked rugs, 20, 21–25

fabric, 21–23
    frame, 23–25
    scissors, 25
    for latch-hooked rugs, 93–95
        backing canvas, 93–94
        latch hook (tool), 95
        yarn, 94–95
    for natural dyeing, 195
    for rya rugs, 80–81
        backing foundation, 80
        needles, 80–81
        pile gauge, 81
        yarn, 81
        yarn quantity, 81
    for woven rugs, 177–178
        frame loom, 177
        shed sticks, 178
        shuttle, 178
        warp threads, 178
        weft, 178
Ethnic origins
    Navajo, 114, 132–133
    Polish, 190–191
    Russian, 176
    Scandinavian, 78–91
    Ukranian, 192, 193
    Yugoslavian, 184
Fabric
    for braided rugs, 62
    for hooked rugs, 21, 22–23
        attaching to the frame, 28–29
        mechanical cutting machine for, 22
        preparing, 25
        quantities, 23
        transferring designs, 28
        washing the fabric, 23
        width of strips, 23
        yarn, 23
    pen wiper rug, 77
    for rya backing, 80
    See also Yarn
Finishing the rug, 199–202
    binding, 200–201
        corners, 201
        edges, 200–201
    blocking, 199–200
    care, 202
    fringe, 201–202
    joining, 200
    lining, 202
Flannel, use of, 22
Folk Art of Rural Pennsylvania (Lichten),
    14
Folk Arts of Norway (Stewart), 79
Frame loom, 177
    rya square on, 181
Frames, for hooked rugs, 23–25
French knot, 77
Fringe, 201–202
    attaching with crochet hook, 201–202
    how to make, 201

Geometrics, 26, 49–50
Ghiordes (rya) knot, 181
    how to make, 82
Goldenrod (dyestuff), 197

Hand hooks, 20
    guiding yarn or fabric with, 29
    how to use, 29–30

Harnesses, 175–177
Hit-or-miss pattern, 26–27
  in blocks, 26
  border, 27
  runner, 27
Hooked rugs, 15–59
  combination of braiding and, 71, 73
  designs, 25–28, 34–60
    antique, 19, 38, 40–47, 50–51, 54–57, 60
    borders, 27
    braided round (antique), 60
    creating your own, 25–27
    geometrics, 26, 49–50
    hit-or-miss, 26–27, 38, 39
    keeping it simple, 27
    leftover fabric (using up odds and ends), 38, 39
    rag rug, 19
    rags (through burlap), and left uncut for background, 16
    stair runner, 27, 59
    stair runner with matching rug, 36–37
    transferring onto foundation fabric, 28
  equipment, 21–25
    fabric, 21–23
    frame, 23–25
    scissors, 25
  foundation (backing), 21
    attaching to frame, 28–29
    preparing, 25
    transferring design onto, 28
  frames, 23–25
    simple type, 24
    size of, 23
    on a stand, 25
    on wheels, 24
  history of, 15
  methods of hooking, 15–20
  piles, 22–23
    mechanical cutting machine for, 22
    quantities, 23
    washing the fabric, 23
    width of strips, 23
    yarn, 23
  procedures, 29–34
    checking the back, 34
    directional hooking, 33
    finishing up, 34
    by hand (traditional method), 15–20, 29–30
    punch hooking, 20, 30–32
    ripping out, 34
    shuttle hooking, 20, 32–33
    tappenalen, 20, 33
    where to start, 33
  tools for, 20

Increase (in crocheting), 144
Increase (in knitting), 163
Interlocking gobelin stitch, 112–113
Iron surfate (mordant), 195

Jack loom, 177
Joining, 200
Jute, 21

Knit stitch, 162
Knitted fabric, use of, 22

Knitted rugs, 160–173
  designs, 163–173
    with diagonal rows, 169
    reversible rug, 170–171
    with vertical rows, 168
  fringe, 201–202
  history of, 161
  procedures, 161–163
    binding off, 163
    casting on, 162
    decrease, 162–163
    increase, 163
    knit, 162
    purl, 162
    slip stitch, 163
Knitting (soumak) stitch, 111–112, 113
  embroidered rug designs for, 126–127

Lacing braids together, 68–69
Lamb's tongue border, 27
Latch hook, 95
  technique of using, 95–97
Latch hooked rugs, 92–105
  designs, 97–105
    antique, 102, 103
    for child's room, 104, 105
    to enlarge, 99
    rya effect, 97
    tongue-shaped pattern, 97, 98
  equipment, 93–95
    backing canvas, 93–94
    latch tool, 95
    yarn, 94–95
  history of, 93
  procedures, 95–97
Latex backing, 202
Lichten, Frances, 14
Liebetrau, Preben, 13
Lily of the valley (dyestuff), 197
Lining, 202
Long-legged cross-stitch, 111, 113

Maple (dyestuff), 197
Marigold (dyestuff), 197
Masking tape, 109
Medina-Sidonia, Duke of, 161
Methods and procedures
  braided rugs, 65–69
    to braid, 65
    for changing colors, 67
    for increasing, 69
    lacing, 68–69
    modified square turns, 66
    oval rug, 66, 67
    round rug, 66, 67
    square knot, 69
    square rug, 67
    starting to braid, 65
  for finishing, 199–202
    binding, 200–201
    blocking, 199–200
    care, 202
    fringe, 201–202
    joining, 200
    lining, 202
  hooked rugs, 15–20, 29–34
    checking the back, 34
    directional hooking, 33
    finishing up, 34
    by hand (traditional method), 15–20, 29–30

    punch hooking, 20, 30–32
    ripping out, 34
    shuttle hooking, 20, 32–33
    tappenalen, 20, 33
    where to start, 33
  knitted rugs, 161–163
    binding off, 163
    casting on, 162
    decrease, 162–163
    increase, 163
    knit, 162
    purl, 162
    slip stitch, 163
  latch-hooking, 95–97
  for natural dyeing, 195–196
    for background colors, 196
    color sources (chart), 197–198
    with common onion skins, 196
    equipment, 195
    and exposing to the sun, 196
    how to begin, 195–196
  pen wiper rugs, 77
  rya rugs, 82
  rya weaving, 180–182
    cutting the yarn, 180
    ghiordes knot, 181
    number of picks between each row of knots, 181
    variations, 182
    working with a butterfly, 180
    wrapping warp edges, 181
  stitches (crochet), 142–144
  stitches (embroider), 109–113
  weaving, 178–180
    carrying thread along the side, 180
    removing from frame, 180
    selvages, 179
    starting a new thread, 179
    weft inserted on the diagonal, 179
Monk's cloth, 2-ply weave, 21
Mono canvas, 107
Mordants, dyeing, 194–195

Navajo Indians, 13–14
Navajo motif, 114, 132–133
Needlepoint designs, 114–125, 128–131, 134–139
Needlepoint Workbook of Traditional Designs, The (Felcher), 113
Needles
  for canvas work, 108
  for the rya, 80–81
Nettle (dyestuff), 197

Onion (dyestuff), 197
Oriental Rugs in Colour (Liebetrau), 13
Oval rugs, braiding, 66

Paraffin wax, 21
Pen wiper rug, 76–77
  backings, 77
  designs, 76, 77
  sewing the circles together, 77
Penelope canvas, 93–94, 107
Picks, 175
Pile gauge, 81
Polish wall hanging (woven), 190–191
Pomegranate (dyestuff), 197
Pressing with wet towel, 202
Privet (dyestuff), 197

Procedures. *See* Methods and procedures
Punch hooks, 20
  adjustable, 20
  how to use, 30–32
  proper position for holding, 32
  rubbing with paraffin wax, 21
  threading, 31
Purl, 162

Rag rug, hooked, 19
Rice stitch, 111, 113
Round rug, braiding, 66
Rubberized backing, 202
Rudenko, S. J., 13
Rug warp cloth, 2 ply weave, 21
Rugs
  in colonial America, 14
  historical background of, 13–14
  See also types of rugs
Runner
  braided, 74
  hit-or-miss, 27
Rya rugs, 78–91
  designs, 83–91
    wall hanging, 90, 91
  equipment, 80–81
    backing foundation, 80
    needles, 80–81
    pile gauge, 81
    yarn, 81
    yarn quantity, 81
  ghiordes knot, 82
  history of, 79
  procedures, 82

Saffron (dyestuff), 198
Salt (mordant), 195
Scissors, 25, 108
Selvages, keeping neat and straight, 179
Shed, the, 177
Shed sticks, 178
Shuttle hooks, 20, 178
  how to use, 32–33
  proper position for holding, 32
Simple woven rugs, 174–193
  designs, 183–193
    nineteenth-century (Ukranian), 192, 193
    peasant (Russian), 176

square, triangle, and circle, 185
    wall hanging, 184, 190–191
  equipment, 177–178
    frame loom, 177
    shed sticks, 178
    shuttle, 178
    warp threads, 178
    weft, 178
  introduction to, 175
  mechanics of weaving, 175–177
  procedures, 180–182
    carrying thread along the side, 180
    cutting the yarn, 180
    ghiordes knot, 181
    number of picks between each row of knots, 181
    removing from frame, 180
    selvages, 179
    starting a new thread, 179
    variations, 182
    weft inserted on the diagonal, 179
    working with a butterfly, 180
    wrapping warp edges, 181
Single crochet stitch, 142, 143
Slip stitch, 144, 163
Soumak (knitting) stitch, 111–112, 113
  embroidered rug designs for, 126–127
Square knot, 69
Square rug, braiding, 67
Stewart, Janice, 79
Stitches
  crocheted rugs, 142–144
    chain stitch, 142
    decrease, 144
    double crochet, 142, 143
    how to begin, 142
    increase, 144
    single crochet, 142, 143
    slip stitch, 144
    yarn over, 142, 143
  embroidered rugs, 109–113
    basketweave, 110
    compensating for extra width and height, 113
    continental, 109
    cross-stitch, 111, 113
    long-legged cross-stitch, 111, 113
    rice stitch, 111, 113
    soumak (knitting) stitch, 111–112, 113

knitted rugs
  casting on, 162
  decrease, 162–163
  increase, 163
  knit, 162
  purl, 162
  slip stitch, 163
Storing, best method of, 202
Sumac (dyestuff), 198

Tappenalen, 20, 33
Tin crystals (mordant), 195
Tools. *See* Equipment
Transferring designs, 28
Tweeds, use of, 22

Ukranian woven rugs, 192, 193

Vikings, 15
Vine, leaf, and flower border, 27

Warp, 13, 175
  on a frame loom, 178
Warp threads, 178
Washing the rug, 202
Weaving
  mechanics of, 175–177
  procedures, 178–180
    carrying thread along the side, 180
    removing from the frame, 180
    selvages, 179
    starting a new thread, 179
    weft inserted on the diagonal, 179
  See also Simple woven rugs
Weft, 175, 178, 179
White birch (dyestuff), 198
Wool fabric, use of, 22, 62
Woolen fabric, sources for, 62
Woven rugs. *See* Simple woven rugs

Yarn
  cutting, for rya weaving, 180
  for embroidered rugs, 108
  hooking with, 23
  for latch hooking, 94–95
    cutting and winding, 95
  rya, two-ply, 81
Yarn over, 142, 143
Yugoslavian (rya and woven) wall hanging, 184